Dwain,

DRIVEN BY DESIRE

INSATIABLE LONGINGS - INCREDIBLE PROMISE - INFINITE GOD

THOMAS FITZPATRICK

The desires that exist deep
in your heart have been
placed in you by a God who
wants you to experience love, joy,
fascination & greatness in ways
you can't even begin to imagine.

Thomas

Published by White Blackbird Books, an imprint of Storied Publishing

Copyright ©2020 by Thomas Fitzpatrick

Permission requests and other questions may be directed to the Contact page at www.storied.pub.

Unless otherwise indicated, Scripture quotations are from the ESV Bible (The Holy Bible, English Standard Version), copyright 2001 by Crossway, a publishing ministry of Good News Publishers. 2011 Text Edition. All rights reserved.

ISBN: 978-1-951991-09-8

Cover design by Sean Benesh

CONTENTS

FOREWORD

This book is dedicated to all of the people who have stuck by me through the ups, downs, highs, and lows of my life and ministry. My desires have driven me to do some things I am so very proud of and some things I am totally ashamed of, but you all have been there every step of the way.

From my closest friends, to all of the amazing students I have had the pleasure of ministering to over the years, to my incredible family (especially my beautiful wife and kids), to a God who has been so faithful to me even though I haven't always returned the favor—I hope the following words and ideas make you proud and help you become more like Jesus.

Nearly twenty years ago, I was given a small paperback book by a student named Nate called *The Seven Longings of the Human Heart* by Mike Bickle and Deborah Heart.

That book changed the course of my life forever.

I hope and pray that my "take" on that material will do the same for you.

Driven by Desire fleshes out what it calls "the feeling of being fascinated by God." Easy to read and provocative, it achieves a balance between making scriptural concepts both conversational and approachable—with the awe of discovery of some of its lesser-known truths about human desire.

Latayne C. Scott
Author, *The Mormon Mirage, Protecting Your Child From Predators, A Conspiracy of Breath,* and over two dozen other books.

Thomas writes in the same way that he speaks and lives— with passion, conviction, honesty, and of course, some humor sprinkled in. As you read this book, your spirit will be liberated to explore what our truest desires are and how they are fulfilled in the fullness of God. Driven By Desire is full of one power-packed chapter after another, and everyone who reads it will discover why God has placed certain desires deep within their heart. This is a perfect book to engage in small group discussion and personal spiritual growth.

Linda Truschke
Campus Minister, Pepperdine University

Thomas Fitzpatrick is a man of passion and fervor for the Lord. This book is an outpouring of that love and zeal. May all of us drink in the words flowing from the Lord through these pages for the transformation of our souls.

Lance C. Hahn
Senior Pastor, Bridgeway Christian Church

My first thought upon reading this engaging book was, "Wow, I can't wait for my children to read this someday." Coming from a Christian culture that emphasized total depravity over *imago Dei*, I have continually fought to understand why on earth God made me the way he did, and what he expects from me in terms of using my gifts and desires for his glory. *Driven by Desire* will be a tool in the hands of God to explain people to themselves and to call us to a full, impassioned view of God's love and intentions for us.

Jessica Ribera
Author, *The Almost Dancer*

Everyone is motivated by something that emanates from the core of their being. It could be recognition, power, or a close relationship. If you want to go through a workshop on the desire that drives you or sort out the value system that is running your life below the surface, this book will be the therapy of sorts. Thomas Fitzpatrick taps deeply into the human spirit for the purpose of directing it to the Holy Spirit. The book is an invitation to a process that will be worth your time.

Christopher Collins
Associate Professor of Higher Education, Azusa Pacific University

Scripture reveals that God tempts no one, but each person is lured and enticed by his own desire leading to sin and death. Is this the full story when it comes to desire? In *Driven By Desire,* Thomas Fitzpatrick shows us that this is not the chief end of desire. God has so much more intended when it comes to desires, and he actually will give you the desires of your heart as you delight in the Lord. This book will help you make sense of what powerfully motivates you from day to day.

Kevin Thumpston
Author, *Questions of the Heart*
Pastor, Watershed Fellowship

If you heard someone say, "Don't deny your desire," you'd expect that to come from Vegas. Thomas Fitzpatrick, however, gives that charge standing on Scripture. He is seriously suggesting that your seven base desires are gifts of God, and they are driving you toward your best life, not your own sinful desires dragging you down to debauchery. In his own words: "Could it be it possible that the great God of the universe specifically created us with these seven desires so that through them, we might actually come to experience and know him?" If he's right, that changes everything.

Mark E. Moore
Pastor, Christ's Church of the Valley
Author, *Core 52: A Fifteen-Minute Daily Guide to Build Your Bible IQ In a Year*

Thomas Fitzpatrick is the real deal. A godly man, husband, father, and pastor. The Lord has used him in a variety of levels of leadership, including through this book. At every page, you will find yourself relating to the illustrations, stories, and struggles. Fitzpatrick offers strong Biblical guidance on how to rightly handle and enjoy the desires that God has given you. I wish I would have written this book, but he beat me to it.

Jared Bridge
President, Baptist Convention of New Mexico
Church Planter and Founding Pastor, Anchor Church

COCOA PUFFS & CRANBERRY SAUCE

Beauty. Power. Intimacy. Adventure. Devotion. Love. Influence.

Sounds like I'm describing a new Netflix series, right? Throw in a few zombies, cowboys, or alien creatures (or a strange combination of all three) and you have yourself a binge-worthy show.

Those words aren't a description of the newest Hollywood hit. They are actually a description of the core longings of the human heart—the core longings of *your* heart.

Look back over that list. Those seven desires are the primary driving force in your life—from the good stuff (the stuff you post online, brag about, and share with the world), to the bad stuff (the stuff you hesitantly tell your closest friends or roommates about late at night), to the really ugly stuff (the stuff you hope no one ever finds out about).

Everything, and I mean *everything*, comes back to one of those seven desires. From what you watch, to who you date, to where you work, to what you do for fun, to how you spend your money, to what apps you download or what games you play, to what degree you choose, to what you tell yourself when you look in the mirror—all of it is driven, at one level or another, by your desires. Beauty, power, intimacy, adventure, devotion, love, and influence are at the heart of everything you do. And that's a problem, especially if you are a Christian.

Most of us assume (or we have been taught by some nice, little, old lady who taught our Sunday school class as a kid) that our desires are bad. We have been told, time and time again, that our core desires annoy God at best or anger him at worst. And thus, if we want to please the Lord, we must turn away from the things that burn deep in our hearts. "Deny your desires" is the message and mantra that many of us have lived by for years.

But is that true? Is that possible? And is that what God actually wants us to do? Could it be that the great God of the universe specifically created us with these seven desires so that through them, we might actually come to experience and know him?

Think about that. And while you do, let me tell you a little story; a story about an eighteen-year-old punk kid named Thomas Fitzpatrick. He had a lot more hair on his head than he does now. He also had a lot more skill on the basketball court.

At the age of eighteen, I was driven by desires that burned deep in my heart and pushed and pressed me to do some pretty crazy things.

- I desired to be known, valued, and loved unconditionally.
- I desired physical and emotional intimacy without

the guilt or regret that always came along for the ride.

- I desired positions of influence and power, and I desperately wanted to be a big deal.
- I desired excitement and adventure, and I wanted to push myself and my body to the limits.
- I desired to be wholeheartedly devoted to something and to feel like I gave it my all.
- I desired to see and behold true beauty (in others, the world, as well as in the mirror).
- I desired to live a life that mattered, one that the world would not easily forget.

Can you relate? Do you not feel the powerful pull of these desires on a daily basis? Whether we recognize it or not, we are all driven by these desires at some level.

But then something happened to me. I met Jesus.

Although meeting Jesus brought such clarity, hope, and joy into my life, if I'm completely honest, it also complicated things a bit.

For one reason or another, I started to believe that all of the passions and desires I had before I met Jesus, passions and desires for things like beauty, power, and intimacy, were... well, evil. Very evil. I assumed that the desires that were deep in my heart for the last eighteen years were all selfish and sinful and now that I was "born again," I needed to separate myself from the passions I was originally born with. I came to believe that there was no place in my new life for my old desires. Books, sermons, and devotionals about "dying to self," "not succumbing to the flesh," and being transformed from my "old way of life" only added to my fears and frustrations.

Although turning away from those desires sounded relatively easy, (I can do all things through Christ, right?) it was anything but. When it came to getting rid of my deepest desires—I couldn't do it! Those desires were an inseparable part of who I was. I couldn't just flip a switch and remove them from my life. I had been driven by those desires for as long as I could remember, and I couldn't find a way to just stop desiring them.

But…

- I asked God to remove my desires.
- I repented of and tried to turn away from my desires.
- I took captive any and every thought that pertained to my desires.

I did everything I could to live in such a way where my desires were no longer the primary driving force in my life. I gave it my best shot, but nothing worked.

Those seven desires were an inseparable part of who I was. Attempting to rid myself of those desires felt as if I was trying to rid myself of being an incredibly funny, good looking, Caucasian, man. Sorry, that's just who I am and who I am always going to be. But in all seriousness, as a new Christian, I believed I would please God to the degree that I disregarded and denied my core desires.

You can imagine the struggle (and the shame) that ensued. Chances are you've felt the exact same way: "I'm a

Christian. But I'm driven by these seemingly 'sinful desires.'" Now what?"

Products Versus Promises

Every day we are inundated with products, pills, promotions, and procedures that all try to answer the "now what?" question for you. All of those things claim they will satisfy our heart's deepest desires.

Click here. Buy this. Try that.

And yet, no matter how many things we buy, achieve, order, digest, inject, slap on, or smear in, it seems as if we always want more. From the student who is never satisfied with his or her GPA to the young executive who is never satisfied with the bottom line. From the athlete who feels he or she has never accomplished enough to the woman who feels like she is never pretty enough. The desires that drive us seem somewhat elusive and insatiable. More, more, more.

Perhaps I can explain it a different way. Most of us feel as if the desires that exist deep in our hearts are like a set of random keys we found in the kitchen junk drawer one day. They look and feel really important, but we have no idea what to do with them. We have no idea where they go or what they unlock. So we aimlessly try every lock we can, growing increasingly frustrated every time they don't fit.

But what if God actually gave you those keys because he wants you to unlock something truly amazing? What if those keys, the deepest desires of your heart, are in fact a way to experience the fullest, most abundant, Christ-centered life? What if those keys were given to you to reveal and then release the very power of God in and through you?

Suddenly those keys aren't frustrating. They become the most critical piece of our faith. Knowing where the keys go and what they unlock might be exactly what you need to enter into a completely different reality. Every page in the rest of this book is dedicated to showing you just that.

Although most of us assume that our desires annoy God or that we must repent of these desires in order to please God, the Bible makes it clear that our desires were given to us by God! He is the one who originally gave us this particular set of keys, and he is the only one who knows exactly what we are supposed to do with them. God teaches us about and draws us closer to Himself through our desires, not in spite of them.

Don't just take my word for it. Listen to what the psalmist says: *"You open your hand and satisfy the desires of every living thing"* (Ps. 145:16).

Did I just hear you right, God? Did I just hear the Holy Scriptures talk about desires? My desires? My seemingly selfish and "sinful desires"?

I didn't believe this verse was correct the first time I read it, so I kept searching. And there, in the middle of the same psalm, as if God knew I was going to doubt this truth, it appeared again: *"He fulfills the desires of those who fear him; he hears their cry and saves them"* (Ps. 145:19).

God fulfilling *my* desires? God hearing the cries of *my* heart? God saving me from the mess I made of *my* life?

I kept reading and sure enough there it was a third time: *"Delight yourself in the Lord, and he will give you the desires of your heart"* (Ps. 37:4).

You don't mean my desire for intimacy, do you Lord? You don't mean my desire for greatness, do you God? You aren't talking about the desire to be fascinated, are you Father? Those are the desires you are going to satisfy within me? No way, no how, no chance. You must be talking about my desire for prayer or holiness or sharing my faith or starting a non-profit where I build homes or love on orphans in some third world country—those are the godly desires that I should have and the desires that you are going to satisfy, right?

Maybe.

But maybe not.

The Depths of Desires

Pastor John Piper said it this way: "The human heart has been and always will be a ceaseless factory of desires." [1] *A ceaseless factory*. Think about that. Your heart is constantly manufacturing desires. It never stops. It runs 24/7/365. Try as hard as you want to shut the factory down or to slow down its production rate, but nothing is going to work or be sustainable.

As I studied the Scriptures, I began to see that perhaps I don't have to try to shut the factory down! Maybe my desires are actually from God and are the very things that will ultimately lead me closer to God! Maybe having those desires is what it means to be made in the image of God. Maybe those desires are the very fingerprint of God on my heart and in my life. Maybe that is how he has uniquely created me. Maybe that is what it means to not only be saved by God, but to actually be satisfied by/with/through/in God! I think it's far more than a "maybe." It's a Biblical guarantee and promise from God himself.

Think about it. It makes perfect sense that a beautiful God would make beautiful creatures that long to behold and become even more beautiful. It makes perfect sense that a loving God would make loving creatures who long to experience the depth and wonder of love. It makes perfect sense that a great and powerful God would make creatures that desire to be great and powerful.

God didn't create us with these seven desires and then say, "Now I want you to spend your life erasing the very image I created you in." That would be a sick game. And it's a game that other religions actually force you to play. Well, no thanks. I'm not interested.

That's why I love the invitation of Jesus. Christianity is not about running away from or ridding yourself of these desires. It's about running to the God who graciously gave us those desires. That small difference will make all the difference in the world. At least it did for me.

In Isaiah 29:8, we read about a man who dreamed all night about eating a great meal but awakened to find that he was actually starving to death. What he thought was real and satisfying was anything but. And the very same thing is happening to a vast majority of us, both Christian and non-Christian.

That's why I absolutely love what we read in Isaiah:

Come all who are thirsty, come to the waters; and you who have no money, come, buy and eat. Come, buy wine and milk without money and without cost. Why spend your money on what is not bread, and

your labor on what does not satisfy? Listen, listen to me, and eat
what is good, and your soul will delight in the richest of fare. (Isa.
55:1–2)

- Why did I feel so empty after I had "my fill" when
  it came to sex and physical intimacy?
- Why did I want more alcohol or marijuana even
  after I'd consumed enough for five people?
- Why did my heart long for more even though I
  was already in amazing positions of leadership
  and influence?
- Why was my GPA or list of accomplishments
  never impressive enough?
- Why did my material possessions lose their luster
  less than a week after buying them?

According to the prophet Isaiah, all of that was true
because I was wasting my time and money on things that
couldn't possibly fill me up. Sex, success, and stuff were not
real "bread" and thus couldn't possibly satisfy my heart and
soul. And yet, that's exactly what I hoped would happen
every time.

The problem is not with the presence or depth of our
desire. The problem is that we typically seek fake, empty,
destructive, and counterfeit forms of satisfaction to these
desires. As C. S. Lewis stated, it's our tendency to settle for
mud pies in the street instead of sandcastles by the sea. Our
mistake lies not in the intensity of the desires that we have,
but in the fake and fleeting ways that we try to satisfy those
desires.

You and I are far more than material beings, thus we will

never fully be satisfied by material things. Let me repeat that phrase because it might be one of the most important in this entire book: you and I are far more than material beings, thus we will never fully be satisfied by material things.

And God knows that because he made it that way. So right in the middle of our mess, right in the middle of our chaos, right in the middle of our hunger pains and pursuit, God says, "Feast on me! I open up my hand and gladly satisfy every single desire of your heart. Stop eating junk food, stop eating scraps from the world's table, come and feast on me—the One, true, unchanging, eternal God."

So when God calls us to die to self or to deny self, I don't think he is asking us to die to desire. He is calling us to die to the selfish, fleeting, and prostituted ways we typically go about satisfying those desires. To die to self-imposed, self-created, self-sustained forms of satisfaction to our desires. To find great delight and satisfaction in him, the only true, pure, eternal, unending source of satisfaction.

It reminds me of Thanksgiving. One year when I was about eight, I woke up on Thanksgiving morning and for some reason, I forgot what day it was. So, as was my custom every morning (then and now), I poured myself an enormous bowl of Cocoa Puffs, and I began to stuff my face with those little chocolate balls of bliss. As soon as I was done with my third bowl, my mom walked into the room carrying my favorite holiday dish of all time—homemade cranberry parfait. She put it on the table and said, "I hope you are hungry. I made an extra bowl of this just for you!"

I can't even begin to describe the desolation that set deep in my heart. I had chosen to go "Coo-coo for cocoa puffs" instead of "coo-coo" for Mom's cranberry parfait. I had stuffed myself with junk food that was easy to find, when the most incredible dish had just been specially made for me.

That very same thing happens all of the time with our desires. We go coo-coo for all the things around us, instead of Christ.

In the Beginning ... Was Desire

Think back to Adam and Eve in the garden.

What made the first couple in human history disobey and completely disregard the Lord? What made them fall victim to the enemy's lies and eat the forbidden fruit? What made them think, "Who cares what God said, let's do it anyway?" Genesis tells us:

> *And when the woman saw that the tree was good for food, and that it was delightful to look at, and a tree to be desired in order to make one wise and insightful, she took some of its fruit and ate it; and she also gave some to her husband with her, and he ate it.* (Gen. 3:6 AMP)

It sounds like the fruit itself and the promises behind it struck a chord deep within Adam and Eve's hearts. The fruit spoke to their desire for beauty (it was delightful to look at), as well as their desire for power, adventure, and influence (it could make you wise and insightful). It appears that Satan knew he could use Adam and Eve's God-given desires to destroy them. It happened then, and it continues to happen today.

The problem isn't in the desires themselves. Beauty, wisdom, insight, intelligence, adventure, etc., were clearly present before the Fall. The problem was where (and in what ways) Adam and Eve sought to satisfy their desires. They didn't need Satan's fake promises or fleeting offers. Neither do we because no matter how many forbidden trees we eat from, the desires still burn deep within us. So much so that, like Adam and Eve, we end up destroying ourselves or others. Siding with and seeking satisfaction from Satan and his schemes always ends up backfiring.

We don't need more trees or more fruit or more of the enemy's empty promises. We need something satisfying enough that will actually match the depth in which we feel these desires. God claims to be and offer just that.

I tried for years to turn away from these desires. I'd pray, "God, make it so that I don't want to be in positions of influence anymore. Make it so that I don't hunger for intimacy anymore. Take away this longing and desire for greatness. I'm a Christian, I shouldn't want something like that." I was asking God to change who he was and who he created me to be.

I in no way want to deify our desires. Our desires are not God, and we do not worship God just so we can get what we want from him (I sing a few worship songs to you on Sunday, God, and you make me more powerful or beautiful on Monday. Good deal).

But what a glorious God we serve. He made us to be like him and invited us to find satisfaction through him.

How Deep Do They Go?

Desires.

What are yours?

How strong are they?

How have you been trying to satisfy them?

And are your desires strong enough, do they burn deep enough to forsake and disregard all of the cheap imitations of the world and to seek true satisfaction in the Only One in whom it can be found?

Let's find out.

———————————————————

1. John Piper, *Desiring God: Meditations of a Christian Hedonist*, (Colorado Springs, Colorado: Multnomah Books, 2017), 12.

STINKY FACE

LOVE

Love songs. Where would the world be without love songs? Whether it's Elvis Presley's "I Can't Help Falling In Love" (go ahead, curl your lip) or Whitney Houston's "I Will Always Love You" (go ahead, shout it out!). From Ed Sheeran's "Perfect" (go ahead, shed a tear) to Lady Gaga's "I'll Never Love Again" (go ahead, keep crying), our lives are definitely happier and sappier because of songs like these. And my sincerest apologies if I just put a certain tune in your head that you will now be singing for the next three days.

Songs are one of the primary places where we see (and hear) evidence of our next desire. But we also see it in ...

- The magnetic pull of popular shows like *Friends, This is Us, Downton Abbey,* or *Stranger Things* (what's an alien invasion without a preteen love story?)
- The fact that romance novels continue to earn the most money every year ($1.44 billion in sales last year—I'm writing in the wrong genre!)[1]

- The amount of money spent every year on
  Valentine's day (\$19 billion)[2]

Our next desire is seen, heard, and portrayed just about everywhere! We even see it in children's books. One night my oldest daughter handed me a book called *I Love You Stinky Face*. The book goes something like this: a Mother is putting her young son to bed when he begins to ask a series of "what if" questions. What if I was a slimy monster? Would you still love me then? What if I was an alien creature? Would you still love me then? What if I was a smelly skunk called "stinky face?" Would you love me then? What if I moved back home after college and lived in your basement until I was 35? Would you still love me then?

Okay, that last one wasn't actually in the book, but it's a great question and deserves an answer!

But the little boy's questions, along with all of the songs, shows, and spending that I mentioned before, attest to a desire that burns deep in the human heart—the desire to be loved unconditionally.

Although mentions of it seem to be everywhere, love itself is actually pretty hard to define, especially when it comes to unconditional love. From poets to psychologists, producers to your parents, many people have spent a lot of time trying to define and/or explain what love is.

Here's my best shot at defining it: the desire to be loved unconditionally is the desire you have for someone, anyone, to love you with all of their heart even after knowing all there is to know about you (especially all the bad stuff).

Your desire to be loved is the desire you have to be wanted and valued based on who you are and not on what you bring to the table or how well you perform. This is the desire you have for someone to show you affection and support without any reservations, hesitations, or limitations. This is the desire you have for someone to give you their best after you have shared with them your worst.

This is the desire you have to be accepted and embraced even though you are a stinky face.

Can you relate to this desire?

A few years ago, a guy out in Maryland started something called PostSecret, a community project where blank postcards were placed on park benches. The cards had a few simple instructions: draw or depict your deepest, darkest secrets and then anonymously mail the cards back to him.

And people did—a lot of people. As you can imagine, a significant amount of the cards dealt with some pretty serious stuff. There were cards with issues of sex, body image, and abuse. Some cards dealt with people who broke the law or their commitments. But more than anything, the postcards talked about the desire to be loved. If you go to the PostSecret website you can see some of these things for themselves—but be forewarned, the things people confessed are as real and raw as it gets. Honestly, that entire art project looks and feels like an adult version of *I Love You Stinky Face*.

The desire to be loved unconditionally—despite our mistakes, failures, and inadequacies—is quite possibly the deepest desire that exists in the human heart.

Run And Hide

Because we all want to be loved so badly, we actually end up doing some pretty bad things.

First, like Adam and Eve in the garden, we hide. Once we come face to face with our own imperfections; once we feel the sting of shame, stupidity, and selfishness; once we have done hurtful, hateful things that we would never tell anyone except a complete stranger on a postcard, we run and hide. Our secrets scare us, and we rightly assume they will scare others.

So we hide. From ourselves. From others. And we try our best to hide from God. In Genesis 3, we read that Adam and Eve tried to cover-up their mistakes by covering up their private parts. They tried to hide behind some sort of makeshift outfit and some handcrafted façade. And if that wasn't enough, then they went and hid out in the bushes too (thinking, "I bet God won't find us here!")

They were embarrassed. They were ashamed. They were afraid. And they felt ugly and unlovable. So they did what they thought was best. They hid. They were "naked and afraid" long before it was a cable TV show!

And don't we do the exact same thing? We don't dress up in fig leaves or hide in bushes, (and if you do I know some great counselors that might be able to help), but most of us hide behind something—our titles, our stuff, our social profiles and online image, our degrees, our hobbies, our families, even our faith. Those are nothing more than twenty-first century fig leaves.

Most of us are just as afraid as the very first couple in the garden was, so we do exactly what they did—we live tentative, timid, guarded lives where we hide our true selves and hesitate to let others in, especially the Lord. We live a life of half-truths, pretending things are A-OK all the while covering up the fact that nothing could be further from the truth. We desperately want others to love us, so we hide the parts of our lives that look and feel unlovable.

If we don't hide, then we hope.

We hope and pray that someone will take notice of us or that someone will stop and actually pay attention to us, that they won't accept the "I'm good, thanks for asking" robotic tagline. And although hoping someone will notice us doesn't necessarily sound like a bad thing, it is. Here's why: we become addicted to affirmation, however fickle or finite it may be. We do everything we can to catch someone's eye and to get attention. We need to feel loved by someone, in some way, so we give ourselves away sexually, or we get all amped up when our most recent post gets more likes than the others, or we dress a certain way so we can attract a bit more attention from a member of the opposite sex (or the same sex), or we cling to every little bit of praise or applause that we can get. And through it all, we assume that when someone notices us or likes something about us, they are somehow or in some way actually in love with us.

But:

- The coaches love you until you get hurt and can't play anymore.
- The "bros" love you until you choose to hang out with a girl instead of spending time with them.
- The girls love you until someone more attractive comes into the room.

- The love you feel from your parents is solid until one night you walk in and hear them throwing around the word divorce and "I don't love you anymore!"
- The boss loves you until a new recruit can do your job in half the time and for half the price.

Naked and afraid. Afraid and ashamed. Ashamed and alone. These are nasty combinations that can dominate and destroy your life. Maybe you can relate. Maybe you can't, not yet.

Maybe you thought if you got a 4.8 GPA, or became president of the club, or captain of the team—that your parents would finally be proud of you, but you found out that nothing is ever going to be good enough for them. Maybe you thought others would love you when you threw caution to the wind and decided to try things you swore you would never do, but now you realize that the moment you stop doing those things, the love will stop as well. Maybe you thought he would love you after you had sex with him, but instead he actually lost interest in you. Maybe you thought if you could just get married, the void for love would be filled, but you've quickly discovered that two miserable people make one really miserable couple.

The desire to be loved has an extremely dark side to it. This desire causes us to do some pretty nasty things and to go to some pretty crazy extremes. We either hide from others or we do things with the hope that others will take notice of us.

Wait A Second!

And therein lies the problem. When it comes to love, we always tend to look to another human being to shower us with that which we so desperately desire. We tend to look to people to show us that we are lovable. Which makes sense.

But everybody you are looking to is actually looking for the very same thing!

How in the world could someone who is just as hungry, desperate, and driven by the desire for love possibly give you what he or she doesn't have? How could that person give you what they need and what they are looking for? How could any person share with you the things they are searching for?

Other people can't really help you because they don't have what you need. It would be like a broke college student asking another broke college student to pay off their student loans. They have enough debt of their own. They can't pay yours too!

The American rapper Post Malone said it well in one of his recent songs, "There's no way I can save you, because I need to be saved too." That is true in so many ways, but especially when it comes to love. You won't have much luck looking to another broken, incomplete, insecure human being who needs love just as desperately as you do to satisfy this desire.

You have to look to God.

In 1 John, we read something incredible:

Whoever does not love, does not know God, because God is love.
This is how God showed his love among us: He sent his one and only

Son into the world that we might live through him. This is love: not
that we loved God, but that he loved us & sent his Son as an atoning
sacrifice for our sins." (1 Jn. 4:8–10)

Think about that for a second. That text doesn't say God
is looking for love or just able to show you love. It doesn't
say he is loving or even that he is in love with love. It says
he is the source of love. He is the epitome and essence of
love. And thus, he is the only one who can truly and forever
satisfy your desire for love. Because he doesn't need it. He
isn't looking for it.

He is it.

He will always and forever give out and give away his
love.

And he actually delights in doing just that, even when
we are at our worst.

The apostle John doesn't say God loved us because we
were lovely or worthy to be loved. He says the exact opposite. The text implies (and others clearly state) that God
loved us when there was nothing lovely about us. He loved
us when we desperately needed help and had no hope. He
loved us when we were hiding from him. He loved us when
we discarded and disregarded him. He loved us when we
were covered in ridiculous fig leaves and stuck in the
bushes.

Because God is love. When he shows up, you get love.
And nothing that we did (or ever could do) will stop God
from loving us. We read this in Jeremiah 3: *"The Lord*
appeared to us in the past, saying, 'I have loved you with an ever-
lasting love'" (Jer. 31:3).

An everlasting love—that's what we want. That's what

we need. That's what we desire. God's love for you is the fullest, most complete, most unconditional love you can imagine. It's true and real and what you were made to enjoy for all of eternity.

No other religion claims that you are loved unconditionally. Not a single one. All other religions exist on some sort of "good enough"/earn it/merit-based system. In those religions you have to work for love. You have to arrive, perform, work, and do things that are lovely or that make you lovable.

But not in Christianity. Christianity has the audacity to claim that the God of the heavens and the earth loves you no matter what—even when (and especially when) you are at your worst. You don't have to hide. You don't have to cross your fingers and just hope. You don't have to highlight your successes and cover up your failures. You can know with absolute certainty that you are loved *unconditionally*.

Go ahead and cover yourself up. Go ahead and hide in the bushes. Go ahead and fake it. Go ahead and share your deepest secret on some postcard. Go ahead and run away from The Lord. Go ahead and do any (or all) of those things, but keep in mind that God loves you—just the way you are! We see that in the Garden. And we see that throughout every page in the rest of the story. God loves you, and he will never stop.

AND ... AND ... AND ... AND

Here's the thing, though: I bet that most of us have heard that truth before. I would bet that most of us have heard someone say (whether a parent, youth minister, friend, or even a complete stranger), "God loves you."

But I'm not sure many of us have ever truly *experienced* the enormity of that truth. We have heard the words, but we've never experienced the wonder behind them! Because if you had, then you would honestly never be the same again. God's love is something that messes you up (for the better, but it still messes you up). It's something that envelopes, excites, and empowers you. It's not something you simply give intellectual consent to (Oh yes, God loves me—check. Next question.). It's something that is intended to radically change you.

God's love is designed to impact you like that stupid little pickled jalapeño pepper impacted me one day at the sandwich shop. I didn't order it. I didn't see it there. But then, WHAM! out of nowhere I was a changed man (I won't go into detail about the changes that I am referring to). God's love is meant to slap you in the face and knock you to your knees. It's not just something you are supposed to agree with or accept.

And we all know people who "get it." We all know a Christian (or two) who honestly believes that God loves them in a very special way (I'm not talking about that guy who thinks he is God's gift to women either). I'm talking about people whose faith is so different and so much deeper than ours, those whose faith is so vibrant and exciting and contagious. Know someone like that?

In my experience in ministry, I would say that nine times out of ten, the primary difference between that person and the rest of us, is his or her understanding of (or better yet amazement of) God's love. If you aren't very motivated in your faith right now, if you aren't really growing in your faith right now, if you are having trouble sharing your faith right now, I imagine that what the Righteous Brothers said years ago applies perfectly to you—you have lost that loving feeling!

For most of my Christian life God's love was a concept that I considered. It was not a conviction that deeply changed me.

Then something happened. And I'm not exactly sure I could pinpoint when or how it happened, but something happened where God's love went from being a part of my life to the very essence and core of my life. The best way I can sum it up is to say that God's love went from an "or" type of love to an "and" type of love. And that change, however small and insignificant it may seem, changed everything.

Think about the importance of the word "and" over and against the word "or." Nuts *and* bolts. Sweet *and* sour. Wet *and* wild. Change the "and" to an "or" in any of those combinations, and you have something very different (and most likely pretty lame). *And* is better. And (did you see what I did right there?) did you know that this particular truth pertains to God's love? AND is better!

God's love for us is so deep and so beyond our under-standing that he has to use the word "and" over *and* over *and* over again to describe it. The only way to adequately explain the love he has for each and every one of us is to compare it to every significant expression of love that we have for one another.

Think about the love relationships that are a huge part of our life.

The Love Of A Friend

Friendship love is a huge part of our world. From bromances like Harry and Lloyd in *Dumb & Dumber*, to animated friendships like those in *Toy Story* (and yes, I cried in the last one, and I know you did too!), from National Best Friend's Day, to friend requests on Facebook (hello 1307 friends!), we see hints and expressions of this type of love everywhere.

There is a great scene in one of the new *Star Trek* movies that powerfully portrays this type of love. Kirk is slowly dying in some glass chamber. Spock is standing helplessly behind the wall. The music gets intense. The camera zooms in. And the two friends touch hands through the glass, Vulcan salute to Vulcan salute. #precious.

But there is just something about friendship love—something about someone who is not related to us in any way, who is willing to go out of their way, to walk with us along the way. Friendship love is a powerful and life-changing type of love. And one of the most amazing things about our God is that he loves us in this way.

We read about this in the Bible:

Oh, for the days when I was in my prime, when God's intimate friendship blessed my house. (Job 29:4)

Greater love has no one than this: to lay down one's life for one's friends.... I no longer call you servants, because a servant does not know his master's business. Instead, I have called you friends, for everything that I learned from my Father I have made known to you. (Jn. 15:13,15)

The God of the universe loves you in the same way your

best friend loves you—a friend that knows you inside & out, a friend that has been with you through thick and thin, a friend that laughs at your corny jokes when no one else does.

God loves you as a person loves their closest friend. When Jesus told his disciples that he no longer called them servants or workers or even students, but friends—he was taking their relationship to an entirely new level. Friends choose us. Friends enjoy us. Friends defend us. Friends help us. Friends like to be with us. Friends bring out the best in us. And guess what? That's exactly how God feels about you.

But this type of relationship, this type of love, doesn't adequately describe the entirety of God's love for you. God also loves you with the love of a friend AND the love of a Forever Father.

The Love Of A Parent

I thought I knew what love was before I became a father, but boy was I wrong. After my sweet girls came into my life, everything I knew about love changed. Even though they cried (okay, screamed) all hours of the night, or cost me lots of money, or dirtied their diapers in the most inopportune places and at the most inopportune times, I loved them with all of my heart—more so than I thought I could ever love another human being.

There isn't a single thing that my girls could do that would cause me to stop loving them. Nothing. I absolutely mean that. Even if they changed their names or walked away from their faith. Even if they went on some ridiculous spree and hurt hundreds of other people and themselves. If that happened, there would definitely be pain, sadness, and separation (and possibly some prison time), but there would always be love. I will always and forever love them—no matter what—because I am their father.

You see, my children are mine. They are my very flesh and blood. And thus, as long as there is still blood running through my body, I will love them. Come heaven, hell, or high-water (not sure what that last one even means, but it sounds dramatic) I will love my children. That's the love of a Father. That's the love of a dedicated daddy. And that's the type of love God has for us.

Several years ago, the world was introduced to Dick and Rick Hoyt. Rick was born in 1962 as a quadriplegic with cerebral palsy. In the spring of 1977, at the age of fifteen Rick told his father that he wanted to participate in a five-mile benefit run. Far from being a long-distance runner, Dick agreed to push Rick in his wheelchair. They finished all five miles, coming in next to last. That night, though, Rick told his father, "Dad, when I'm running, it feels like I'm not handicapped." This realization was just the beginning of what would become over one thousand races completed, including triathlons (six of them being Ironman competitions), and biking and running across the entire US in 1992, completing a full 3,735 miles in 45 days.

What would compel a man to do something like that, to go to that extreme and endure that type of pain?

The love of a father for his child.

What would compel a grown man to die on a cross? What would compel him to shed his blood and give up his life? What would compel him to go to that extreme and endure that type of pain?

The love of a father.

Listen to how God describes his love for you in 1 John: *"See what great love the Father has lavished on us, that we should be called children of God! And that is what we are"* (1 Jn. 3:1).

God loves you as a father loves his own children. God, the maker, sustainer, and savior of the world, loves you with the love that a daddy has for his daughters (or his sons). It is a never changing, never in question, never in doubt type of love.

And knowing that should change everything.

The story is told about two men in a coffee shop who were talking about the strictest judge in town. One of them said, "I bet there's not a single person in this whole county who doesn't fear that man!" A small little voice from behind them piped up and said, "I'm not afraid of him." The two men laughed as they turned around to see a small six-year-old boy stuffing his face with a cinnamon roll.

"Oh really," one man said. "And why not?"

Without looking up or skipping a beat, the little boy said, "Because he's my dad!"

You see, when you know who your dad is, when you know how much your dad loves you, when you know how devoted your dad is to you, then all fear and worry and anxiety are removed from the equation. Knowing God loves you like a great father should love you means you cannot exhaust his love or do anything that would cause him to stop loving you.

If God loved you like I love queso dip, then I would be worried. That's not real love (although I really do love queso). That's not the deepest expression of love. That's not unconditional love. That's just a short-lived, fleeting, attraction. My life doesn't depend on queso (at least that's what the counselor keeps telling me). God truly loves you like his life actually depended on it. Because he loves you like a faithful, forever Father.

When teaching us to pray, Jesus said, "Father...." That's all he needed to say because that says it all! God loves us like a faithful friend AND like a dedicated daddy.

But that love, even as deep and good as it is, cannot fully and completely describe God's love for you. And that's why Jesus also says that God loves us with the love of a spouse.

The Love Of A Spouse

Listen to what the prophet Isaiah writes:

> *As a young man marries a young woman, so will your Builder marry you; as a bridegroom rejoices over his bride, so will your God rejoice over you.* (Isa. 62:5)

God loves you with a *PS I Love You* kind of love; with a *Notebook* kind of love, with *A Gone with the Wind* kind of love. He loves you with the love of a heroic husband.

This is the kind of love that grips and stirs our heart. The movie *Up* depicts this type of love better than anything I have ever seen. Without even uttering a single word, the opening scene of the movie portrays a love we all long for. (If you aren't bawling like a baby within the first five minutes of that film, then something is seriously, seriously wrong with you!) A man and a woman committed to one another since childhood. Sharing all of life's ups and downs, highs and lows. Serving each other and making great sacrifices for one another. Dreaming together and even walking through the valley of the shadow of death together. That is love at its very best.

There is a reason we get all emotional and teary when we watch something like that—because we were created to enjoy and experience something just like that. You long for that love because you were made to enjoy and experience that type of love!

Let me try to say it a different way. A Scottish preacher named Billy Wilson once told me this, and it changed my life forever: "She wore my sweatshirt, even though it didn't fit her at all. It looked foolish, even ridiculous on her. She shouldn't have been wearing it in the first place, but she wasn't wearing it to make a fashion statement. She wore it because it was mine."

Think back to the different ways we show and express love to our romantic interests over the course of our lives. Right now my daughter Tori shows love by giving kisses, but for her a kiss is a slobbery open-mouthed assault (for the sake of future dating relationships, we hope she grows out of that). In elementary school, we show love by chasing people around the playground or maybe writing love letters that ask something like, "Do you love me? Check yes or no!" In middle school, we write the name of the person we love all over our binders. We stick notes in their locker during passing period. And of course, there are middle school dances, where every once in a while a few brave soldiers venture across into enemy territory, some never to be seen again.

Then there is high school. In high-school you talk on the phone all hours of the night, "You hang up, no you hang up. I love you more, no I love you more." And then my personal favorite: "She wore my sweatshirt, even though it didn't fit her at all. It looked rather foolish, even ridiculous on her. She shouldn't have been wearing it in the first place, but she wasn't wearing it to make a fashion statement. She wore it because it was mine.

After working at a little hole-in-the-wall restaurant for nearly three months when I was in high-school, I finally saved up enough cash to buy this one Tommy Hilfiger sweatshirt that was at the mall. A few months into our relationship, my girlfriend at the time (a girl who now just happens to be my wife), asked if she could wear my sweatshirt. Now ladies, that's like asking a man for the keys to his hot rod or the remote control to his TV. My sweatshirt? My Hilfiger sweatshirt? The most expensive, precious, important thing I own?!

Well, she had my heart, so I handed it over. And many of us have experienced this very same thing, whether it's a sweatshirt, a jersey, a t-shirt, or even a letterman jacket. They are all four or five sizes too big, but we choose to wear them anyway. Why? To gain the approval of others? To make a fashion statement? To look cool?

No, we do it for love. That's what love does. 2 Corinthians 5:14 says that love grabs you by the neck and forces you to do things you wouldn't otherwise do. And so we rock the jersey, we sport the coat, and we wear the jacket because we love the person to whom they belong. We want to be as close to that person as possible, so we take their things, and we claim them and we wear them as our own.

Now I need you to hear something. And if you aren't paying 100 percent attention, then just put the book down and walk away. You have to hear this, really hear this.

Are you ready?

The Creator of the Universe loves you with all of his heart. He loves you like a spouse loves his better half. He loves you like a googly-eyed groom loves his new bride! Don't believe me? Don't believe that his love for you is that passionate and intense and meaningful?

He bore the cross, even though it didn't fit him at all. It looked rather foolish, even ridiculous on him. He shouldn't have been wearing it in the first place, but he wasn't wearing it to make a fashion statement. He wore it because it was mine.

Let that sink in for a minute. He wore it because it was *yours*. He wanted to be as close to you as possible, so he took what was yours and wore it as if it were his own.

You wouldn't die on a cross for a pet. You wouldn't sacrifice your life for a lab rat. You wouldn't breathe your last breath for a business partner or even a long lost relative. You would only make the greatest sacrifice of laying down your life for the person you love more than any other. And that's how God feels about you, and that's why he did what he did.

God loves you like a faithful friend AND like a dedicated dad AND like a heroic husband. And, and, and, and.... It appears as if our longing to be loved unconditionally is matched only by God's desire to love us in that way! Like I said before, AND is always better.

I love my family with all of my heart, and yet the love I have for them is limited and tainted by my humanity and sinfulness and selfishness. But not God's. God is able to love us in all of these ways and then some. He is holy and pure and good, and thus the love he showers on us is the same.

So in your pursuit to find satisfaction to this desire, I pray that you will stop hiding, and even stop hoping, and instead start delighting in the truth that you are loved, unconditionally, by the God of the universe.

And that is true, even if you are a stinky face!

Drive This Desire Home

To drive this desire home, I challenge you to try one of the following things.

Be Honest

In what ways do you hide from others? Take a few minutes to think about the mistakes, decisions, thoughts, experiences, and struggles that you keep from the people around you. From that thing you did last summer, to that thing you think about doing each night, to that person you wish you could do something with—what are you hiding? Once you answer that question, go one step further—why? Why are you hesitant and afraid to share those struggles, temptations, and regrets with others? Do you think those thoughts, mistakes, or experiences make you unlovable?

If you aren't hiding from others, maybe you are desperately hoping others will notice you or just take an interest in you. Do you find yourself dressing a certain way in the hopes of getting a few looks? Do you find yourself acting a certain way in the hopes of getting a few laughs? Do you find yourself doing certain things in the hopes of fitting in or even standing out? Take a few minutes and process all of this with God in prayer. We all want to be seen, known, and loved. In what ways are you trying to make that happen?

Put A Name To It

As it pertains to love, spend a few minutes and write down the names of a few people who have shown you love throughout your life. From parents, to friends, to a spouse, list the people who have shown and expressed love for you. Take it one step further and write down a few ways in which they have shown you love. What did their love look like? What made it so good and so meaningful?

Personalize The Word

Pick a few verses in Scripture (a few examples would be Zeph. 3:17, Ezek. 16:4–14, or Luke 15:11–32). Read them over, but as you do, insert your name into the pronouns. Put yourself in the shoes of the original characters and audience. Act as if the Lord is saying those truths directly to you. Because he is!

Enjoy The Lord

I want to challenge you to spend more time with the Lord. You can go big and try to find a three-to-five-hour block in the next few weeks to be with God (just be fore-warned, you might fall asleep during that chunk of time and/or get totally bored, but I promise that crazy things tend to happen when you give God that much of your time). Or, just carve out three five-minute intervals throughout the next few days.

- Give God your first five minutes in the morning (whether through reading, praying, worship, or even silence—and no, hitting the snooze button doesn't count)!
- Give God some time halfway through your day (reflect on what has already happened and pray about what is yet to come).
- Give God your last five minutes (tell the Lord how the day went, and what you enjoyed and what you did not—and even if you start to snooze during this one, I'm pretty sure that the One who loves you like a friend and a father and a husband is just fine with you falling asleep in his arms).

Stand Firm In His Love

Your enemy, the devil, can't stand the thought of your being safe and secure in God's love. That's why he is going to have you question it and doubt it all the time. You get a bad grade on a test, or fail on the field, or give into a temptation and you think, "What's wrong with me?" Which then morphs into "Why am I such a screwup and a failure?" Which then morphs into "No one would ever love this mess. I am such a fake and a fraud." It always starts off

small, but then it quickly turns into a self-condemning accu-
sation about your inherent worth and value. All of that is
the enemy trying to undermine the love God has for you.

But Romans 8:38 tells us that nothing can separate us
from the love of God. NOTHING. Which means that even
your own stupidity can't separate you from the love of God.
Think about that. Even your addiction to porn can't separate
you from the love of God. Even the tendency you have to cut
yourself or hurt yourself can't separate you from the love of
God. Even the nasty things you believe to be true about
your body or the mistakes you have made in the past, or the
people you have hurt, or the lies you have told, or the
bushes you have hidden in—none of it can separate you
from the love of God. Nothing can. His perfect, unending,
unconditional love for you is intended to drive out all fear (1
Jn. 4:18). So if and when the enemy tries to tempt you into
thinking you aren't loved, stand tall in the realization that
nothing could be further from the truth. You are loved by
God. Always and forever. No matter what. Unconditionally.

---

1. Mahogany Turner-Francis, "Book Genres That Make the Most Money."
   Bookstr, November 20, 2018. https://bookstr.com/article/book-genres-
   that-make-the-most-money/.
2. Kimberly Amadeo, "Shoppers Feeling the Love This Valentine's Day."
   The Balance, February 7, 2020. https://www.thebalance.com/happy-
   valentine-s-day-retailers-feeling-the-love-3306043.

THE BIG (AWKWARD) SEX TALK
INTIMACY

L et's start this chapter off by playing a little word association game. I am going to throw out a certain word, and I want you to shout out whatever comes to mind. Don't worry, there are no wrong answers here, but just remember, there might be women and children present!

First word: *Chipotle* (go ahead, say it!)
How about: *Tom Brady* (okay, don't say it!)
Next: *The Kardashians* (I can't believe *I* just said it!)

All right, let's do one more, but this time keep your thoughts or answers to yourself (please and thank you): *intimacy*. What words or phrases come to mind when you think about the word intimacy? Be honest.

If you Google search this particular word (something I don't suggest you do with little ones around), the first and quite possibly the only thing that pops up are three little letters... SEX. For a vast majority of people intimacy=intercourse. But that association is shallow and incomplete. Let me show you.

Did God Just Say That?

Right smack dab in the middle of the Bible towards the end of the Old Testament is a book of Hebrew love poems that are so erotic in nature that young Jewish boys were once forbidden to read them (all of my younger readers just suddenly became a bit more interested in the Old Testament). These poems make up the book Song of Solomon.

And although most of us wouldn't consider that particular book to be X-rated, the material in that book does in fact deal with intimacy in a rather erotic manner. But the fact that God chose it to be part of the Bible is important—very important. It means we shouldn't shy away from this conversation. Through the poems in the Song of Solomon, along with several other key texts in the Bible, God has given us incredible insight into our desire for intimacy. And although some might call this conversation the "awkward sex talk," it's one that we need to have—especially with our Heavenly Father.

One day a little boy asked his mother where he came from and she proceeded to tell him a tale about a beautiful white-feathered bird. The boy asked his grandmother where his mom came from. Again, he received a variation of the bird story. One day on the playground he told his friend, "You know, there hasn't been a normal birth in our family for three generations."

When it comes to intimacy, it's easy for us to complicate or convolute things. But that isn't necessary. In the Song of

Solomon, we read about a relationship between a young man and a young woman. It all starts when they first meet and continues until they get married. But through that developmental process, the book goes into great detail about the complexities, joys, and thrills of being with another person in an intimate way.

Like most young men, the guy in these poems is pretty obsessed with the woman's body. He goes on and on about how beautiful she is and how amazing she looks. Although if I were to use some of the same language that he did with my wife ("Your legs are like the trees of Lebanon"), I'm not sure it would have the same effect that it did back then.

The woman is gracious in receiving the comments and even reciprocates the passion on occasion. But several times throughout their relationship, the woman in the book says, "Do not arouse love until the proper moment" or "Do not arouse love, until it so desires."

That's an interesting thing to say and definitely not a response that you hear today. Her words—"Do not arouse love until it so desires"—are incredibly insightful and instructive. Here's why. The woman is telling her man, the one who can't stop drooling over her, that what they have is so beautiful and so good. But if they are not careful, if they take things too fast, too far, or do things out of God's designed order, they will end up making a mess out of it all.

A few years ago the country music group Lady Antebellum (now known as Lady A) came out with a song that speaks directly to this. It's called "Just a Kiss" and in the song they say, "I don't want to mess this thing up, I don't want to push too far...."

Mess things up.

Push too far.

When it comes to intimacy that is exactly what a lot of us have done. Luckily, God has designed us for so much more.

What Are You Talking About?

Let's make sure that we are all on the same page here as we start having this conversation. Dictionary.com defines intimacy this way:

> Intimacy—A close, familiar, affectionate, loving personal relationship with another person that is based on detailed knowledge and deep understanding.[1]

In chapter one, we talked about our desire to be loved unconditionally. In this chapter we move from love to intimacy. And although they are very similar, they are also very different.

- Love— the desire to be accepted, valued, and deemed worthy in the eyes of another.
- Intimacy—the desire to enjoy, embrace, and experience a deep, meaningful connection to another.

As is the case with all of our desires, you can't repent of, ignore, or act like you aren't driven by your craving for intimacy and connection. It just boils down to where and how you will seek satisfaction to this particular desire.

That's One Way to Do It

As my Google search for the word "intimacy" proved, a vast majority of people assume or allow their desire for intimacy to drive them into the bedroom. Although that is an option, it's not the answer to all of our intimacy questions or the solution to all of our intimacy problems.

I want to get real here for a minute: having sex with someone can be a singular expression of intimacy, but it is far from the entirety of it.

Nothing in the definition of intimacy explicitly involves sex. Look again.

Affection for another

A detailed knowledge about another

A deep understanding of another

A close connection with another

That might include sex, but it's not primarily based on sex. Physical touch and physical affection might be a byproduct of an intimate relationship, but they are not the only product. That's where most people go wrong. Most people assume that when you can get someone to sleep with you, then you will somehow satisfy this craving for intimacy. But the opposite is in fact true. If you only experience intimacy on a sexual level, then you will probably end up missing out on everything else—like an affectionate, detailed, deep connection.

Now I'm not saying that "your sexual urges are from the devil, you little heathen," or that "Christians, even after they are married, should wear giant onesies at night and sleep in separate beds" (it helps if you say all of that in a crotchety old person voice, BTW).

No, sex is a gift of God, a very good gift in fact...WHEN it is viewed and treated as a singular expression of intimacy and not as the entirety of it. In our world, sex is not a just small part of the intimacy equation, it is the entire thing—from start to finish. A vast majority of us have come to believe that satisfaction to this particular desire only happens in/through sex.

And If You Call Now...!

Do you know why most people equate intimacy with intercourse? Do you know why we are so sex-obsessed and sex-crazed? Do you know why we think intercourse is the answer to all our intimacy issues?

Because sex sells.

From cars, to burgers, to hotels, to movies—sex sells.

In 2018, *Avengers: Infinity War* brought in $1.7 billion, making it one of the highest grossing films of all time. But listen to this. In that same year, the cumulative profit for porn videos in the US was (are you ready?) $10.65 billion. Eight times that of the most successful Hollywood movie.

Let's stay on the numbers and statistics train a bit longer. In 2018, Microsoft reported profits in excess of $100 billion. ExxonMobil, the world's largest publicly traded company and number five on Forbes' top 2000 companies, posted 2018 profits of $20 billion. But, in that same year the sum of international revenues from pornographic videos, sexual novelties, magazines, "dance" clubs, pay-per-view, and Internet was approximately $120 billion. That's larger than the annual revenues of the NFL, NBA, and MLB combined!

"Choo, choo!" Keep the train coming.

Last year, Americans spent over $1,000,000 on Viagra and slightly under $1,000,000 on Cialis—pills designed to enhance your sex life and help guys perform better in bed. Strip clubs in California alone bring in annual revenues of $1 billion; strip clubs in the US bring in annual revenues of $3.1 billion dollars a year, and strip clubs around the world bring in a paltry $75 billion annually. Retailers that sell lingerie, nightgowns, "shape-wear" and other specialty items made $11.8 billion in 2012.

Do I need to go on? Sex sells.

A lot of different people have found ways to sell you a lot of different things—all for a very large profit. They have convinced you that your desire for intimacy (as well as your desire for love, power, and fascination) will somehow be satisfied in/through physical, sexual experiences. So we pay to have sex, or we pay to enhance our sex lives, or we pay to watch sex, all because we have literally bought into the lie that intimacy=intercourse.

I just have one little problem with all of that (okay, I have a bunch of problems with all of that) but the biggest issue is this: if intimacy is intercourse, then why are the most sex-crazed places also the most lonely, desolate, and desperate places out there?

Think about Amsterdam's Red Light District, Las Vegas' strip clubs, or even the prostitute downtown. In all of those situations—situations where sex runs rampant and where intercourse is commonplace—people are empty, alone, and completely broken. But wait, shouldn't the sheer amount of sex they are having leave them completely satisfied? So much more so than the rest of us?

Not exactly.

- You can buy sex, but you can't buy a deep understanding.
- You can buy porn, but you can't buy detailed knowledge.
- You can buy intercourse, but you can't buy a close connection or true intimacy.

In fact, you can be having sex, a lot of sex, even in the context of a Christian marriage, and still not be experiencing intimacy at all.

Yet most of us believe (and buy into) the lie that when we connect ourselves with another person physically, however real or fake or manufactured or fleeting that connection might be, that we will find satisfaction for our desire for intimacy.

Dancing on the Table

Let's imagine that our desire for intimacy is a table (a weird object lesson given the theme of this chapter but go with it for a minute). The top of this table is your connection to another person. It's your desire to know, experience, and understand someone on the deepest levels possible.

Well, like any good table, intimacy is supported by four legs. Jesus tells us exactly what those legs are in the Greatest Command: *"Love the Lord your God* (be intimately connected to God), *with all of your heart, with all your soul, with all your mind, and with all your strength"* (Mark 12:30).

Here in this text God lays out how we were created to connect with him as well as how we were created to connect to others—heart, soul, mind, and strength.

- *Heart*—Your heart represents your deepest passions and emotions, the things that make you happy or sad, that fill you with joy or angst, that make you laugh or feel angry. Your heart is where your desires are birthed and come from (I know a good book about desires if you are interested).
- *Soul*—Your soul is your inner self—your hopes, dreams, fears, aspirations, talents, and memories. Your soul is what makes you, those distinctive qualities and characteristics that tools like the Enneagram speak to (I'm a 7, wing 8 by the way).
- *Mind*—Your mind encompasses all of your thoughts and mental processes. It's what you think about, reflect on, question, ponder, and daydream about.
- *Strength*—Your strength corresponds to your body and the way you use your energy. From working out to passing out, our strength is how we use our frames and physiques.

When it comes to intimacy, most of the world focuses entirely on the physical aspect, the "strength" leg of the table. Most people believe that when they are connected to someone else physically, they will experience the fullness of intimacy and find satisfaction to their heart's desire. But a table with only one leg doesn't look like "the fullness" to me

—it looks like a tripping hazard, bad modern art, or a piece of junk.

What about the other three legs? When it comes to the stability of a table, aren't all four legs equally important? So what about our heart, soul, and mind? If you aren't intimately connected to another person emotionally, then the physical connection you share won't ever be enough. If you aren't connected to another person spiritually, then the physical connection won't actually be that good. If you don't know the thoughts, hopes, dreams, fears, and doubts of another person, then nothing you do in the physical realm will ever be able to compensate for that.

Intimacy, true intimacy, demands that all four legs of the table are equally present. Intimacy is a complete understanding and a deep knowledge of another—on every possible level. And if a person hasn't spent the time to build up and strengthen the other parts of the relationship, then they don't deserve to taste the fruits of the physical part of the relationship. If another person isn't willing to invest in your heart, soul, and mind, then they haven't earned the right to invest in (or experience) your body.

If intimacy only means intercourse for you, then you will never find true satisfaction to your heart's deepest desire because you are just settling for sex (is it okay to drop the mic right now?).

Settling Versus Being Satisfied

All right, climb off the table for a minute, and let's get back into Song of Solomon. As I mentioned before, that particular book gives us a glimpse into a very passionate relationship between two people who are madly in love. Yet, three different words are used to describe their love.

First is the Hebrew word *riyah*. *Riyah* means "friendship" or "companion love." Think "best friend" or "I could tell this person anything." That's *riyah*. The lovers in this book first share and experience this type of love with one another.

From there, they describe their love as *ahavah*. *Ahavah* is a deep affection kind of love. This is love where you can't stop thinking about the other person and when you honestly feel like "I'd rather be with you right now, in this moment, than anywhere else in the world." This is a deep-seeded, heart-felt, committed type of love. In fact, in Songs of Solomon 2:4 and 8:6–7, the two lovers say their *ahavah* is as strong as death." That's pretty intense.

From there, we read about *dode*. The word *dode* means to arouse or to fondle. I don't think I need to go into much detail about the meaning of this word. This is the physical and sexual element of a relationship. The word *dode* is where we get the Greek word *eros* which is the root for our word erotic.

So, you have *riyah* love (friendship), *ahavah* love (devotion), and *dode* love (sexual). Now stay with me. When the woman says they should not arouse love until they are married, ("until the proper time") guess which one she is referring to? You got it—*dode*.

She wants to experience the depths of intimacy with her man. She doesn't just want to sleep with him. She wants to have a deep connection to him, not just have sex with him. That's too easy. That's too surface level. That's selling themselves short. She wants to know him intimately on every level. And if they rush it, or push it too far, or only focus on the physical part of intimacy, then they will mess the whole thing up.

Jesus talks about this when he uses the term "one flesh" to describe a marriage relationship between a man and a woman. Becoming "one" with another is way more than just having sex. It is a connection that includes emotions, hearts, minds, and the very mingling of souls.

The coming together sexually is supposed to be the outworking and manifestation of a much deeper connection that should be happening on so many other levels first. If it's not happening on that deeper level, then when you have sex, you will not be truly satisfied.

Take marital affairs or one-night stands as an example. Two people are experiencing intense and exciting *dode* but without the *riyah* or *ahavah*. There is no friendship, no commitment, and no deeper connection. And thus, the people involved are left feeling empty, unfulfilled, and broken after it all. *Dode* alone will never truly satisfy.

Or how about the married couple that has been together for over twenty-five years and then suddenly gets divorced. There was obviously some *ahavah*, some commitment to one another. But let's be honest, there was probably hardly any *riyah* friendship. And chances are there was little to no *dode*. And thus, as they neglected the different areas of intimacy, they eventually grew apart.

When we only focus on one type of intimacy, no matter who we are or how old we are, when we short-circuit things or believe the lie that intimacy is all about intercourse, we are living outside of God's intended design and allowing the enemy to use this desire to drive us to despair.

Let Him In

But there is good news for those of you who have felt the emptiness of cheap, one sided, unbalanced intimacy. There is good news for those of us who are struggling to find true satisfaction to this desire. There is good news for those of us who have believed the lie (and acted on it) that intimacy primarily comes through intercourse.

The good news is this—God has given us all that we need to find satisfaction to this desire.

First, he has given us marriage. That's why we hold up, value, and seek to strengthen marriages. They are the space where intimacy can be experienced, where all of the different forms and expressions of love come together in a beautiful way. That's why marriages are under such attack—because the enemy knows they are something so sacred.

But more than that, more than just giving us marriage, God has given us himself. Marriage is great and being closely connected to your spouse is amazing, but the God of the universe longs to be intimate with you. And he has made such a connection possible. That connection is the most important and satisfying form of intimacy imaginable.

Think about it. If intimacy is only experienced in marriage (or just through sex), then Jesus never experienced it. If intimacy is only for those who find a mate, then singles, widows, or those who choose to not get married, will never experience the fullness of it. But why would God give this desire to everyone, if only a select few would be able to find satisfaction to it?

The intimacy that God offers transcends all other forms and is available to everyone.

- *But if one loves God truly [with affectionate reverence, prompt obedience, and grateful recognition of His blessing], he is known by God and recognized as worthy of His intimacy and love.* (1 Cor. 8:3 AMP)

- *So when you pray in your private prayer language, don't hoard the experience for yourself. Pray for the insight and ability to bring others into that intimacy.* (1 Cor. 14:13 MSG)

- *There's more to sex than mere skin on skin. Sex is as much spiritual mystery as physical fact. As written in Scripture, "The two become one." Since we want to become spiritually one with the Master, we must not pursue the kind of sex that avoids commitment and intimacy, leaving us lonelier than ever—the kind of sex that can never "become one."* (1 Cor. 6:16–17 MSG)

We can become spiritually one with God in a way that is similar to how we become physically one with another person. We are able to connect ourselves to the very source of all that is good and experience a deep type of intimacy *with him.*

Take a minute and read the words of the great King David:

O Lord, you have examined my heart and know everything about me.

*You know when I sit down or stand up. You know my
thoughts even when I'm far away.*

*You see me when I travel and when I rest at home. You know
everything I do.*

You know what I am going to say even before I say it, Lord.

*You go before me and follow me. You place your hand of
blessing on my head.*

*Such knowledge is too wonderful for me, too great for me to
understand!*

*I can never escape from your Spirit! I can never get away
from your presence!*

*If I go up to heaven, you are there; if I go down to the grave,
[a] you are there.*

*If I ride the wings of the morning, if I dwell by the farthest
oceans, even there your hand will guide me, and your strength
will support me.*

*I could ask the darkness to hide me and the light around me
to become night—but even in darkness I cannot hide
from you.*

*To you the night shines as bright as day. Darkness and light
are the same to you.*

*You made all the delicate, inner parts of my body and knit me
together in my mother's womb.*

*Thank you for making me so wonderfully complex! Your
workmanship is marvelous—how well I know it.*

*You watched me as I was being formed in utter seclusion, as I
was woven together in the dark of the womb.*

*You saw me before I was born. Every day of my life was
recorded in your book.*

Every moment was laid out before a single day had passed.

(Ps. 139:1–16 NLT)

That's detailed knowledge.

That's a deep understanding.

That's intimacy.

And the passages above should cause us to rethink how we view and enter into worship and prayer. Those things are actually the very means by which we experience intimacy with the God of the universe. And that connection, that intimate relationship, transcends all of the other forms that are available to us.

Think about communion. When we take communion, we partake of God in a very tangible, yet mysterious way. We take his body and put him inside of ours. That is a very intimate experience. And yet, it's not sexual.

Or how about baptism? In that act and demonstration of faith we invite God to cover us, infuse us, clothe us. And in that moment, the Scripture teaches that we enter into Christ. Again, extremely intimate, but not sexual.

Or how about the gift of the Holy Spirit, where God promises to enter into us?

The list goes on and on. Intimacy with your Heavenly Father is not only possible. It is the fullest, most complete form of intimacy available to you. It is the satisfaction to your heart's deepest desire. And I honestly believe that until you know that intimacy, all other forms and expressions of intimacy will be rather empty and fleeting. For all of eternity God will say, "That was just the beginning. Come closer. There's more." And he invites us to start now.

So it doesn't really matter what you think of when you hear the word "chipotle" or the name "Tom Brady." What really matters is what comes to mind when you think of the word "intimacy." Because the things you associate with this desire will be the very things this desire drives you to do and pursue.

You don't have to settle for the world's limited definition of intimacy any longer. You don't have to buy into the lie that intimacy always (or only) means intercourse. Instead, you can find true, real, deep, meaningful satisfaction to this desire by connecting yourself intimately to the God who formed and fashioned you in the very beginning. He is the God who sent his Son to die for you, the God who is right now preparing an eternal dwelling place for you that is far more beautiful than you can imagine.

Speaking of beauty, let's go there next.

Drive This Desire Home

To really drive this desire home, I challenge you to try one of the following things.

Define It

Take a minute and write out your own, personal definition of intimacy. Here's the catch—try to define it without using the word sex or intercourse. How does your definition line up with Webster's: a close, familiar, affectionate, loving personal relationship with another person that is based on detailed knowledge and deep understanding?

Break Free

Let's be honest for a second. If statistics are right, then nearly 70 percent of young adults in America are struggling with, if not addicted to, pornography. That particular vice is destroying us (and our experience of true intimacy) in ways we can't even fully fathom. If you find yourself stuck or settling for that fake, cheap, prostituted form of intimacy, I implore you to break free. Here's how I think that process can start. It has to do with our past, present, and future.

Past—spend some time unpacking and coming to terms with your past. When were you first exposed to sex, porn, and/or physical intimacy? Was it a movie? A website? A friend? Was intimacy and physicality a taboo topic in your home when you were growing up or did you talk about it a lot or see your parents model it in healthy ways? Were you introduced to sex in a flippant way, where dad or big brother or sister more or less shared their porn with you? Or worse, were you introduced to sex in an abusive way, where someone took advantage of you? You have to figure out what your history, backstory, and foundations are because they have dictated and determined your trajectory and led you to the place you are now. If sex was dirty, taboo, evil, painful, suppressed, legalistic, etc., for you early on, I imagine porn is incredibly enticing.

Present—spend some time unpacking and figuring out your present-day habits and patterns. We are all, whether we like to admit it or not, creatures of habit. We all follow and fall into certain rhythms, tendencies, and patterns. From what you eat, to how you spend your free time, to when you watch porn. It is imperative that you start to record, and thus more fully own and understand, what that pattern is for you. What time of day (or night) do you typically struggle with this temptation? Where are you when you typically watch it? What was your day like, or what is your mental state, before watching porn (are you typically bored, tired, frustrated, angry, etc.)? Are there certain things (shows, people, or images) that tend to trigger you and tempt you? Understanding how you operate, or more specifically how the enemy typically operates in your life, is key to breaking free from a porn addiction. Once you understand your sin "rhythm," you can be very intentional in breaking the cycle and changing things up.

Future—cling to and fight for the beautiful future that God has in store for you. The Scripture tells us that the devil comes to steal, kill, and destroy. When it comes to a porn addiction, that is true at so many levels, especially as it pertains to your future. Porn has a unique way of destroying the amazing things God has in store for you. Porn wrecks your chances of experiencing real intimacy later. When we become addicted to the fantastical, selfish, aggressive sex that is typically found in porn, we allow the enemy to destroy our minds, bodies, and spirits in such a way that we will not find fulfillment in real, married, God-honoring sex. Countless studies show how porn changes our brains and our bodies. So one of the ways to break free from porn is to believe that in seeking purity you are actually fighting for your future—mainly your future spouse. Every time you turn away from porn now, you are making a huge investment in your future. Every time you seek purity now, you are positioning yourself for the future. What you do right now has huge implications for what your experience of intimacy will be later. Don't sit idly back and let the enemy just take your God-given future from you. Don't let the enemy steal your joy, kill your body and mind, and destroy your experience of intimacy—now or in the future. Fight him. And fight to find true satisfaction to this desire.

Break It Down

Jesus gives us an incredible description of what intimacy looks like when he tells us to *"Love the Lord with all of our heart, soul, mind, and strength."* Has anyone ever loved you in that way? Take a few minutes and write out what it would even look like or feel like to be loved in that way:

- Heart (emotions, feelings, aspirations)
- Soul (hopes, dreams, longings, prayers)
- Mind (thoughts and ideas)
- Strength (actions, time, energy)

Talk About It

To satisfy our desire for intimacy, God has given us two things—marriage and himself.

Let's talk about marriage (you single people, this still applies to you so don't hop on your phone). If you are married, are you seeking to love your spouse in all of the ways listed above? Is he or she working hard to love you in those ways as well? Why or why not? Is your marriage a place where intimacy (on all four levels) is experienced to the fullest extent? What areas are weak? What areas are missing completely? For you single folk, if you are working toward a relationship with someone else, what are your non-negotiables? What are you praying for and looking for? How are you preparing yourself now to love another person in all four of the areas listed above when the time comes?

God has also given us himself. What do those words mean to you? Do you take pleasure in the fact that God knows everything there is to know about you, from your body, to your inner thoughts, to your deepest desires and dreams? Although that causes some people great dread, the Bible seems to think it should bring us great delight. How can you take great delight in the truth that God is intimately aware of and intimately available to you?

Try It

If you are in a relationship with someone that is purely based on sex and physical touch, take a break and take a good, hard look at what is really going on in that relationship and why. Spend some time asking God if you are actually missing out on real intimacy because you are so focused on intercourse. If you have crossed lines and added regrets physically, and if you haven't been pursued or loved on the other three love levels, then it's time to set some boundaries and develop some new patterns and habits. If your relationship can't survive a little less sex, if you can't go a few days or weeks without being together physically, then something might be wrong. The table might be ready to tip over—if it hasn't already.

If you are married, spend the next few days focusing your attention on everything but the physical aspect of your relationship. Talk instead of touch. Look into each other's eyes instead of just at each other's body. Share with one another your hopes, hurts, and heartaches, and don't just hop into bed. Work on strengthening the other legs of your intimacy table and watch how God will naturally bring more abundance to the physical leg as well (sorry, that analogy is getting a little weird now. Let's move on to our next desire)!

---

1. "Intimacy," Dictionary.com, https://www.dictionary.com/.

MIRROR, MIRROR ON THE WALL

BEAUTY

It is probably one of the most famous lines in all of history, right up there with MLK's "I have a dream" or Neil Armstrong's "One small step." It goes something like this, "Mirror, mirror on the wall...." If you are reading this in some super hipster coffee shop with a ton of strangers around you, I dare to say it out loud.

"Mirror, mirror on the wall, who is the fairest of them all?"

The evil stepmother in Sleeping Beauty gets all the credit for giving this phrase to us, but the question she posed actually speaks to a desire that burns deep within us. It's our desire for beauty. Here's how I wish that particular phrase and question ended—"Mirror, mirror on the wall, who gives a flying rip what you say!"

But the truth is that we all do. A lot more than we would like to admit to.

Let me share some interesting statistics that I think will prove my point.

The US has the largest cosmetic market in the world. Statistics report that in the US alone, the beauty industry brought in a whopping $56.2 billion in 2015.[1] Based on estimated percentages, that means:

- $6.5 billion a year is spent on fragrances
- $7 billion a year is spent on makeup
- $8 billion a year is spent on skin care
- $9 billion a year is spent on hair care
- $13 billion on toiletries

As a bald guy, the money spent on hair makes me laugh. Some people pay good money to make their hair blond, while others pay to cover up the blonde. Some pay to have their hair styled, while others pay to make it look like there is no style. Some pay to cut or remove their hair, while others pay to extend or grow it. And that's just hair!

Now don't get me wrong, I'm all for personal hygiene, and I like colognes and shower gels more than most guys, but these numbers seem a tad bit excessive, don't you think?

Americans are ninth in terms of annual per capita cosmetic spending, which equates to around $255 a person every year.[2] Countries like Japan and the Netherlands are just slightly more obsessed than we are, but $255 a year is a lot, especially when you compare it to a place like India which only averages $2 a person.

It seems that every single day people around the world, and especially here, spend a ton of money on Tangle Teezer, tanning beds, tummy tucks, Tory Burch paraphernalia, treatments, or even just tweezers. Every single day, people ask the very same question the evil stepmother did. And because they aren't satisfied with the answer they receive, they slap on, smear in, inject, digest, enlarge, or enhance just about anything and everything that they can.

In addition to the products or procedures we use *on* ourselves, think about the ways in which we use (and abuse) social media to promote or post things *about* ourselves. From the perfect selfie that took thirty minutes to capture and thirteen filters to help make it "perfect," to the innumerable comments we hope to receive about how amazing those selfies are after we post them online, we are all driven by our desire for beauty.

This particular desire has two sides to it.

There is the longing to be beautiful (to be considered handsome, attractive, sexy, or stunning by others) AND the longing to be with or connected to beautiful things (to be seen and associated with beauty).

Every dollar spent, every post we make, every gym membership we sign up for, every piece of designer clothing we purchase, every diet we commit to, every dating app we swipe through, every picture we take (of ourselves or anything else for that matter)—all attest to the enormity of this particular desire. We all want to be beautiful, and we all want to be around beautiful things, objects, and people. Ugliness is not something we aspire to, long for, or want to be associated with.

All of this reminds me of an ad that appeared in a country newspaper. It read: "Farmer wants to marry woman, 35 or older, with tractor. Send picture of tractor."

No matter who we are, we are all drawn to beautiful things. Author Christopher Morley says it this way:"There is a secret nerve in everyone's heart that answers only to the vibrations of beauty."[3] Whether it's the beauty of the moon over the ocean, the beauty of a new bride, the beauty of a child's dimples, the beauty of a perfectly struck golf shot, or the beauty of a nice new tractor, our hearts long for beauty. We want to behold breathtaking beauty, and we want to be considered breathtakingly beautiful as well.

The Beautiful One

And although some of the statistics I shared with you seem outrageous, our obsession with beauty makes perfect sense. Think about the God in whose image we have been created. The prophet and the psalmist both say it perfectly when they wrote: *"For how great is God's goodness and how great is his beauty"* (Zech. 9:17 KJV). And, *"Let the beauty of the Lord our God be upon us, and establish the work of our hands for us"* (Ps. 90:17 NKJV).

Some refer to God as "The Beautiful One," and others call his dwelling place the "throne of beauty." And those in the Bible who were given a glimpse of God were unable to adequately describe what they saw.

Maybe something similar has happened to you. Maybe you have seen something so incredible, so unique, and so beautiful that you literally struggled to find words to describe it.

- Maybe it was a snow-capped mountain range or a sea that was as smooth as glass.

- Maybe it was the smile of a child or the look of pride on a parent's face.
- Maybe it was a beautifully adorned prom date.
- Maybe it was that cookie shake from Chick-fil-A (I know, I have a problem, but don't tell me those things aren't beautiful at multiple levels).

The beauty you beheld was so breathtaking that you struggled to describe it: "It was like this, but it was also like this, and tad bit like this ... but it was so much more than that too!" That's exactly what happened to Ezekiel, Isaiah, and the apostle John when they saw God up close and personal. God's beauty was so intense, so enthralling, and so incredible, that they were unable to put it into words.

This breathtakingly beautiful God made *you*. And not only did he make you, but he made you to be like him! He made you to be beautiful.

Beauty Is Bigger

More than all of our other desires, our desire for beauty (and our fear of feeling ugly) proves that God exists. Beauty is a powerful apologetic for the existence and necessity of God.

If there is no standard, no source, and no starting point, the concept of beauty breaks down into personal preference at best and downright meaninglessness at worst. If everything in the galaxy is an accident, if it is all just part of a random process of mutating cells, if there is no rhyme or reason to anything—then the concept of beauty means absolutely nothing. Things just are the way they are, and nothing is more beautiful than anything else. A healthy child running through a sunlight field of wildflowers is just the same as a malnourished child whose belly is bloated who is about to die in the dirt.

Without God, without a standard or "measuring stick" so to speak, you couldn't call one ugly or one beautiful because that's just the way the chips fell. That's just how the molecules mutated. Things are just things, and they have no inherent worth or value. Thus, I can call really beautiful things ugly (or vice versa) and you couldn't tell me otherwise.

If there is no God, there is no basis for beauty. Things are just things. Beauty implies worth. Beauty implies value. Beauty implies significance. Beauty implies that there is some standard and starting point by which we determine what is and what is not beautiful.

One author's analogy describes it well. Let's say you are standing with a group of friends at the Grand Canyon and everyone is absolutely blown away by the beauty of that place. But then one friend, you know "that guy," says something like, "Eh, it's nothing special. It's just a giant hole in the ground. It's just a bunch of particles that have accidentally fallen into place. I mean what's the big deal?!"

The big deal? The big deal is that *you don't think it's a big deal*!!! We all know that your friend's comments say more about him than they do about the Grand Canyon. That place is beautiful whether or not you or "that guy" (or anyone for that matter) affirms it. And that's true with every beautiful thing.

Beauty is defined and determined by something much larger than us.

That "something" is actually *someone*. His name is God. He is the foundation and the source of all that is beautiful. And thus, beauty is not arbitrary or subjective or random. It is based in the very character and nature of God. So when we call something beautiful, we are actually saying that it looks like, resembles, or exudes the very beauty of God. The opposite would be true for those things that we call ugly. Beauty is based on God and God alone.

Most people believe the opposite to be true. Most people believe that beauty is something that *we* define, something that *we* produce, something that *we* create. Most people think that we are the source and standard of beauty, and thus, we can satisfy this craving if we can just get our hands (or our face or our skin or our hair) on the right stuff.

Says Who?!

Two questions show the idiocy of all of this. The first is: What gives certain people the right to define beauty for the rest of us?

See if you recognize any of the following names: Joanna Coles, Dylan Jones, Gary Vaynerchuk, Marc Cherry, Lee Ann Meriwether, Donald Driver, Shawn Johnson, and retired Army Brig. Gen. Anne MacDonald. Do any of these names ring a bell? Don't worry if not, I didn't have a clue who they were!

These people are more or less the "experts" on all things beauty. Joanna is the editor and chief of *Cosmopolitan* magazine. Dylan runs *GQ*. And the rest were the judges for the 2015 Miss America pageant. I don't have anything against any of these individuals, but like an angsty pre-teen I have to ask, "Who made you the boss of me? Who made you the king of the universe?"

What gives this select group of people the right to define beauty for the rest of us? Who said they are the gurus of what we should consider to be good looking? Why are they the ultimate authority on attractiveness? Tribal chiefs in Africa once claimed that extremely large women were beautiful because it proved they ate well and would live a long life. Young men in Thailand think that the woman with the palest skin is the most beautiful while young men here in the states think that the woman with the tannest skin is the most beautiful. If we let anyone (or everyone else) define beauty for us, we will never be able to truly experience it because it is constantly being redefined.

Shoot, if beauty is up for debate, then I am here to argue that 6' 0" balding, white men with chicken legs and large noses are absolutely gorgeous! They are now the new standard of beauty. Everyone should look like that!

Why? Because I said so. Guys like me are now the fairest of them all! Good luck to all of you who have full heads of hair, calf muscles, and a cute little button nose.

But in all seriousness, a handful of people cannot determine (and should not be allowed to determine) what defines beauty for everyone else. They didn't originally create beauty, and thus they don't have the right to determine what true beauty is. More than that, these so-called experts tend to make a mess out of this particular desire, a mess that the rest of us have to live in and try to clean up. Those who have assumed the responsibility of defining beauty for everyone else tend to do so in incredibly unrealistic ways that deceive and ultimately destroy people. From eating disorders, to self-harm, to the emotional roller coaster we go on every time we try to look as perfect as the billboard model—it is clear that the definition of beauty that many of us are living by is actually really ugly.

Let me ask you a second question: How are all of our "beauty aids" working out for us?

In light of all the products, procedures, posts, and pampering that are available, how beautiful do we feel? How do we see ourselves late at night (or early in the morning) when we stand in front of the mirror? Are all those products and purchases quenching our thirst or satisfying our souls in terms of beauty?

If so, then why are so many girls, especially young girls, so depressed and dejected when it comes to their physical appearance? Why do so many girls hurt themselves, starve themselves, and literally tear themselves apart over their body image? Why are eating disorders, addictions, and suicidal thoughts so common among young women in the Western World?

If we can achieve beauty on our own or through the purchase of some new product, why are so many guys secretly struggling with insecurity? Why are so many dudes embarrassed by their appearance? Why do guys hide behind the weight bench or the designer clothes or the protein shakes trying to convince others, but mostly themselves, that they are attractive and desirable?

Our beauty insecurity is driving us insane! I have known far too many guys who desperately want a beautiful girlfriend to make up for the ugly things that are happening deep inside their heart. I have witnessed far too many women obsess over the attention they can get from the guys because they secretly think they are the ugliest person on the planet.

One student said it this way, "We work so hard to be beautiful, not necessarily so we feel beautiful, but so that other people will think, say, post, or tell us that we are." And it's true. We aren't satisfied with just a few likes or comments or shares. We want hundreds of people to boast about our beauty. I want to be beautiful, and I want/need A TON of people to affirm it. But that desire, and the distorted ways we are trying to satisfy it, are driving many of us crazy.

If we could make ourselves beautiful, then don't you think we would have by now? If we could make ourselves beautiful then don't you think that $255 a year would have done it? How much more is it going to take? $300? $500? We have more beauty aids than any other generation, and yet a vast majority of people in this generation feel so ugly!

Made To Mirror

Here's why. It all boils down to one simple truth: beauty is not something we manufacture. It is something we mirror (look at that last line again—it might be one of the most important and liberating truths you will ever hear).

Beauty is not something we manufacture; it is something we mirror.

Think about the moon. By itself, the moon is more or less just a giant rock caught in the gravitational pull of the earth. There is nothing all that special, unique, or captivating about it. But we have all been amazed by the beauty of the moon. Whether it was a full moon glistening over the ocean, or a small sliver of the moon on a dark, snowy night —the moon is beautiful.

But the beauty of the moon ultimately comes from its ability to reflect the light of the sun. When the moon is at its best, it is simply taking the beauty and light of the sun, something that is significantly more powerful than it is, and reflecting it back to us. The moon is more or less forgotten about (dare I say it's rather ugly), when it is positioned too far behind the world, when it is hidden from the sun, and when it is not reflecting and mirroring the beauty of something greater than itself.

And I think God gave us the moon to teach us one of the most powerful lessons about beauty.

True beauty—breathtaking beauty—is not a matter of buying or applying, enhancing or enlarging, posting or promoting, but a matter of reflecting and mirroring the beauty of God. True beauty, our beauty, is not a matter of smearing on, rubbing in, filtering or editing, but a matter of mirroring back the beauty of God. We become ugly if and when we allow the world to cover us up and when we stop reflecting that which is so much greater, and more beautiful, than we are. Namely, God's Son.

You are not beautiful because of what you see in the mirror. You are beautiful because your life is like a mirror that reflects the beauty of God.

Therein lies our challenge. Christians have to move away from the fake, invisible, moving target that is the world's definition of beauty and into a place where we reflect the eternal and unchanging beauty of God. He is the source of all that is beautiful, and in him our desire for beauty will be satisfied. And although it is easier to apply, buy, filter and

Photoshop, we have all been created to mirror and reflect the Lord.

Let me close this chapter by suggesting two things that I think will help.

Ask God to impart his beauty onto you. Right now, there is a breathtakingly beautiful God sitting on a breathtakingly beautiful throne in a breathtakingly beautiful kingdom. His beauty is not computer-generated. His beauty is not airbrushed or enhanced in any way. His beauty is not fake or fickle. And you are not a shallow person if you want to be beautiful like him. But you have to stop looking at shallow things and start looking at him.

One of the most amazing things about our beautiful God is that he wants to impart his beauty to us! The prophet Isaiah describes this well when he writes, *"The Spirit of the Lord God is upon me, because the Lord has anointed me to preach good tidings to the poor … to give them beauty for ashes"* (Isa. 61:1, 3, NLT).

That is an odd trade, don't you think? Ashes aren't good for anything. They are dirty, messy, and symbolic of ugliness, sin, and death. Ashes are the result of something being set ablaze and destroyed by fire. And if we are honest, our hearts and lives are full of ashes. All that is left of our $255 is a pile of ashes (or half-used beauty aids). From wrecked relationships to scared bodies to cabinets full of cosmetics, all that exists in many of our hearts are the charred remnants of something good.

And that causes us to feel empty and ugly. That causes us to feel unloved and unwanted. That causes us to give up hope. But the glorious news of the Gospel, and the incredible promise of Isaiah 61, is that the beautiful God who originally made us, longs to impart his beauty onto us! Listen to how the apostle Peter said it: *"After you have suffered for a little while, the God of all grace [who imparts His blessing and favor], who called you to His own eternal glory in Christ, will Himself complete, confirm, strengthen, and establish you [making you what you ought to be]* (1 Pet. 5:10).

It doesn't matter what we have done. It doesn't matter what we have tried. It doesn't matter how much time or energy or money we have wasted. It doesn't matter what the mirror says (or doesn't say), the beautiful God of the universe longs to *impart* his beauty and glory onto you. I want you to understand the importance and significance of that word—impart. We allow the world, the enemy, and countless companies to "put" things on us. Things like labels, masks, products, etc. But by it's very definition, when something is "put" on you, it is only impacting you or changing you at a surface level. When something is "put" on you, it can easily, and many times, needs to be removed. So instead of simply putting beauty or glory or blessing *on you*, God imparts those things *to you*. He transfers, bestows, and gives you those things at the deepest levels. The beauty God wants to give to us is not simply skin deep. It goes down to our very core and becomes an intrinsic quality that we possess forever. Don't settle for a fake, fickle, and fleeting beauty to be put or placed on you temporarily. Press into the Lord and ask him to impart true, real beauty into you for all of eternity!

The beauty of God, a beauty that never ends and that will never fade, is transferable through Jesus. Becoming a Christian is about so much more than just being justified before God. It's about being beautified by God!

It's not the fact that we meet or conform to some external criteria that makes us beautiful. It's not that we have the slimmest body, most chiseled six-pack, prettiest face, or most followers. Those temporal things won't ever satisfy us because the standard always changes, and there is always someone out there who is "fairer" than we are. Beauty boils down to us receiving and then reflecting a beauty that comes from God through Jesus Christ. Beauty for ashes. Beauty from ashes.

Why look to Maybelline to make you beautiful, when you can look to your Maker? Why look to L'Oréal, when you can just ask the Lord (and lover) of your soul? Why rely on Cover Girl when your Creator has already promised it to you? Why rely on social media when your Savior's approval is all that matters? It's not about products, procedures, or other people. It's about his promise and his presence!

Just ask Moses.

When you are in the company of your Creator, when you are in the midst of the Majestic, God will transform your countenance and your face. You will begin to look more like him, and everyone will take notice! Moses had to cover up his face after spending time with God back in the book of Exodus because God's beauty started to radiate out of him like the sun. Now I've seen some scary spray tans over the years, but good luck finding a product or a procedure that can cause your face to glow like that.

And in light of what happened to Moses, listen to what the apostle Paul says:

> *Now all of us, with our faces unveiled, reflect the glory of the Lord as if we are mirrors; and so we are being transformed, metamorphosed,*

into His same image from one radiance of glory to another, just as the Spirit of the Lord accomplishes it. (2 Cor. 3:18 Voice)

That's what makes someone breathtakingly beautiful—a face that shines because it reflects and mirrors the very face of God.

But when we ask a beautiful God to make us beautiful like he is, we need to prepare ourselves to go far beyond a few physical improvements or enhancements. And that leads us to our second major takeaway.

Accept that true beauty has very little to do with what we can see on the outside.

The apostle Peter said it better than I ever could:

Don't be concerned about the outward beauty of fancy hairstyles, expensive jewelry, or beautiful clothes. You should clothe yourselves instead with the beauty that comes from within, the unfading beauty of a gentle and quiet spirit, which is so precious to God. This is how the holy women of old made themselves beautiful. (1 Pet. 3:3–4)

We have all heard the words, "It's what's on the inside that counts." And most of us rolled our eyes and disregarded those words because our grandma said them after our face broke out in pimples the day before the big dance. But those words do in fact point to a profound spiritual truth. The truth that our external appearance isn't truly the best measure of our beauty (or lack thereof).

Just ask all of the actors and actresses who in their older age are trying to preserve their outer beauty. I know you spent ridiculous amounts of time and money trying to stay physically attractive, but guess what? It's not working. And that shouldn't come as a huge surprise to anyone—that's what physical beauty does. It dies off, diminishes, and eventually disappears completely. But there is another type of beauty, a beauty that never fades and only gets stronger over time. That's the beauty our hearts truly desire.

Isaiah 53 is a fascinating passage that talks about Jesus: *"He had no beauty or majesty to attract us to him, nothing in his appearance that we should desire him"* (Isa. 53:2 NIV).

What makes Jesus so beautiful? What is it about this man that draws so many people to Him? Why do I have so many pictures of Him hanging up in my office? Was it His great beard? Was it His awesome prayer shawl? Was it His dark skin or His designer outfits? According to Isaiah 53, none of those things mattered at all. In fact, Isaiah says in terms of physical appearance, Jesus didn't measure up. Physically speaking, he was rather normal, plain, and didn't possess any qualities or traits that anyone would get overly excited about.

So what made him so beautiful? What made him so captivating? Isaiah goes on to tell us:

> *Yet it was our weaknesses he carried; it was our sorrows that weighed him down. And we thought his troubles were a punishment from God, a punishment for his own sins! But he was pierced for our rebellion, crushed for our sins, He was beaten so we could be whole. He was whipped so we could be healed. All of us, like sheep, have strayed away. We have left God's paths to follow our own. Yet the Lord laid on him the sins of us all.* (Isa. 53:4–6 NLT)

From God's perspective, nail-pierced hands are far more beautiful than perfectly manicured nails. From God's perspective, tear-filled eyes are far more beautiful than mascara-covered ones. From God's perspective, a broken and bruised body is far more beautiful than a slim, fit, muscular one.

Nail-pierced hands, tear-filled eyes, a broken body. Those are the things God thinks are stunning. And that is what makes Jesus the fairest of them all. It was his radical love for others. It was his willingness to get in the dirt and mess and grime of people's lives. It was his character and humility. It was his commitment to God no matter the cost. It was his obedience to the end. It was his sacrifice, servitude, and self-lessness.

If we want to truly satisfy our hearts desire for beauty, we have to put down the products and pick up the cross. We have to mute the comments of the crowd and tune our ear to the voice of Christ. We have to stop looking in the mirror and start asking God to help us mirror him!

Think about this with me—on Jesus' resurrected body, on the glorious, eternally beautiful body that he had after he rose from the dead—what stood out to everyone? What proved to the disciples that this "ghost" was actually Jesus?

Was it not his scars?

Was it not his imperfections?

Was it not the wounds he had on his hands and his feet?

If it were up to us, we would have asked God to remove those after our death. I mean if there were ever a moment to airbrush something off, or filter something out, it was at the resurrection. Take the nail holes out of the picture, God! But that's not what happened.

Scars, something the world considers rather ugly, were transformed into defining beauty marks. And those same marks will be eternally beautiful—because they are of God, they are from God, and they point people back to God.

And the things in our lives that do the same, are the very things that will make us beautiful, now and for all of eternity.

Let's end this chapter with the words of a man who longed for beauty maybe more than any other. He wanted to be beautiful, he surrounded himself with beautiful people, and he wanted to build beautiful structures. But at some point in his life, he realized all of those pursuits were rather fickle and fake. So he penned these words:

> *One thing I have asked from the Lord, that I will look for: that I may live in the house of the Lord all the days of my life, to look upon the beauty of the Lord, and to worship in His holy house.* (Ps. 27:4)

To look upon the beauty of the Lord. That's where true beauty, real beauty, and everlasting beauty begins and ends —with the Lord. The world desires beauty. Maybe, just maybe, we as Christians have what 55 billion dollars can't buy you—true satisfaction to this particular desire. That's not only true as it pertains to our desire for beauty, but also for fascination and wonder. We will go there next.

Drive This Desire Home

To drive this desire home, I challenge you to try one of the following things.

Take An Inventory

Go through your closet, your bathroom, and your medicine cabinet and start coming to terms with how many beauty aids you have purchased and consumed lately. How do you stack up to the average American who spends $255 a year on cosmetic products and beauty supplies? Are you well below that average, or are you well above it? Why? Or, if products aren't your vice how about posts? How many posts have you made in an attempt to have others affirm your beauty? How many selfies do you need to take or filters do you need to use in the hopes of making yourself look just right? How many comments or likes do you need to feel beautiful?

Come To Terms

Spend some time thinking about the scars or imperfections you have that you try to cover up. From a mark on your face, to a cut on your wrist, to a smaller chest size (that applies to both men and women), write down what "ugly" parts of yourself you try to hide or compensate for. How does the fact that Jesus' purposefully kept his scars and wounds on his resurrected body change the way you see your scars or imperfections?

Answer This

How do you define beauty? Have you ever actually written down or defined for yourself, what makes you (or anyone else for that matter) beautiful? If not, chances are you are trying to hit an invisible, moving target. Write down five to then characteristics of true beauty. Why are certain things on your list and not others? Can the things on your list change over time? How would your list differ from one created by Christ?

Look Closer

Read Isaiah 52:7, Ecclesiastes 3:11, Ezekiel 16:1–22, Matthew 23:27, Matthew 26:6–13, and Revelation 21:2. What does God consider beautiful? What does it mean to be beautiful as you are doing God's work or reflecting God's face? If you stopped asking the mirror, and started asking your maker if you were beautiful, what do you think he would say? How do the verses listed above help you know the answer to that question?

Try It

Ladies, go a week without wearing any makeup. Guys, go a week without shaving. Everyone, go a month without buying any clothes or posting anything on social media. Do what you can to flip your definition of beauty on its head. Push yourself to spend significantly less time, energy, and money on physical beauty aids or self-promotion. Find a way to invest your $255 a year cosmetic allowance on kingdom things and initiatives.

---

1. Beauty Industry Analysis 2019, Cost & Trends, https://www.franchise-help.com/industry-reports/beauty-industry-analysis-2018-cost-trends/.

2. "Prestige Beauty: per Capita Consumer Spending Worldwide by Country 2017." Statista, https://www.statista.com/statistics/1057887/per-capita-spending-on-prestige-beauty-global-by-country/.

3. "Explore Christopher Morley Quotes. QuoteCites.com." QuoteCites, https://quotecites.com/quote/Christopher_Morley_7771.

THAT WAS AWESOME-ISH
FASCINATION

Years ago I was babysitting my best friend's three-year-old daughter down in LA. We went to the park that afternoon, and wouldn't you know it, there, on the side of the hill, was the biggest, scariest looking metal slide I had ever seen. This thing was sixty-feet tall (it might have even been 10,000 feet high now that I think about it).

The little girl I was watching desperately wanted to go down the slide, so against my better judgment, up the hill we went. When we got to the top, I secured her as best as I could between my legs, and then we prepared for takeoff. Some punk high school kid must have put Crisco on that slide because we went flying as if we were shot out of a canon. We were going so fast that even after the slide itself came to an end, our ride did not. We flew off the end of the slide and proceeded to skid across the ground. I did my best to shield the little girl and protect my gluteus maximus all at the same time. When we finally came to a complete stop and the dust settled a bit, my friend's daughter turned to me and said, "That was awesome! Let's do it again, but this time you go down on your stomach, and I'll ride on your back!"

That's called a desire for adventure and fascination. And it's a desire that we all have.

That's why we take things apart and then try to put them back together (sometimes with a few extra pieces lying around). Or we ride the craziest roller coasters we can find. Or travel to new places to see new things and experience new cultures (I'm still not sure what I ate that day in Bangkok). Or drive our cars a bit faster than the authorities say we should. Or go to IMAX 3D movies where we can't even hear ourselves think and where fire comes out of the floor (okay not exactly, but wouldn't that be cool if it did?) Or jump out of planes or off of cliffs.

We want to push the limits and see how far we can go. We want to be amazed, adventurous, and awestruck. From the toddler who stacks books on a chair to get to the cookie jar, to the billionaire who stacks rockets to get other billionaires to the moon—we all, at one level or another, want to be blown away. We all want to be fascinated.

That's why we tend to hold up and idolize athletes. They do things on the court or out in the field that average people can't do. Their abilities amaze us. That's why we flock to the movies and drop small fortunes on snacks, drinks, and a bucket of popcorn. Because Hollywood has a way of expanding our horizons and teasing our imaginations. That's why we consume and purchase so many products. Because there is just something about a cooler car, a faster computer, a larger TV, or a bigger house that excites us. And that's why so many of us are adrenaline junkies and climb mountains, jump out of planes, or strap two pieces of metal to our feet and purposefully point them down a snow-covered hill. We want to experience something, anything, that pulls us out of our comfort zones and pushes us to our limits.

The Dark Side

This desire, though (like all of them), has a dark side to it. A very dark side. To satisfy my desire for fascination, I can fall heavily into debt, buying things I don't really need and actually can't afford. I can fall prey to drug or alcohol addictions because I become hooked on the high those things produce. Or things like pornography become increasingly appealing because in that particular world, the line between fantasy and reality is not only blurred, it is obliterated. Or I can put myself in risky situations, doing things that put my life (and the lives of others) in great danger because when you push the limits, sometimes they push you back—hard.

Despite all of the avenues we can take, all of the experiences we can have, all of the stuff we can try or buy, most of us are still pretty bored. We all sound like my kids on Saturday morning. While standing in the playroom, surrounded by games and activities, they turn to me and say, "I'm bored. There's nothing to do."

And I can't get too mad at them for saying that because I know the feeling.

I've driven fast cars (much faster than my Prius). I've purchased new, shiny, expensive things. I've experienced some athletic success. I've gone white-water rafting and jumped off a cliff or two. I've tried drugs and alcohol. I've been with different women.

But even after all of that, I truly feel like the average teenager who stands in front of a pantry full of food and says, "UH! There's nothing to eat in here!"

Right now, our middle daughter's favorite question to ask is, "Daddy, what do we do now?" Even after I describe the busy day we have planned, she says, "Okay, but what do we do now?" That's a question we all ask.

What now? What next?

After a while, even if I go bigger, faster, more expensive, latest, and greatest, to the limit—I eventually end up at the same place I started. Rather disinterested, disappointed, or dejected. I eventually run out of money, or motivation, or the means to satisfy this particular desire.

And yet, we try so hard to convince ourselves otherwise.

Everything Is AWESOME! Or Is It?

We used to live out in California where everything had to be awesome!

How was your summer vacation? "Awesome!"
How is that new car? "Awesome!"
How is school going? "Awesome!"
How's that book on desire you're reading? "Awesome!"

Everything is awesome (and yes, it's okay to sing that song right now). But think about it. If everything is awesome, is *anything* really awesome? Could it be that we use that word all of the time (or others just like it) because we are trying to convince ourselves (and others) that our life is full of adventure and fascinating things? Is it possible that we claim everything is awesome because we are trying to hide the fact that most things aren't?

Our insistence to use that word proves that, deep down in our hearts, we desperately want things to be awesome. And luckily for us, something actually is.

Pop The Hood

If you pop the hood in your heart, you will find a battery that beats for adventure. We have been hard-wired to seek (and find) enthrallment and excitement in this life. That should make complete sense. A fascinating God created a fascinating world. Then he placed fascinating beings in it who desire to be fascinated. So all of us, whether introvert or extrovert, rich or poor, male or female, Christian or non-Christian, extreme sports enthusiast or couch potato, want to behold and be a part of something incredible.

And there is something out there that fits the bill. It's not *something*. It is actually someone.

When it comes to our desire to be amazed, excited, and blown away in this life, most Christians and non-Christians assume that God doesn't have much to offer. Yes, he "so loved the world." Yes, he sent his one and only son to die for us. Yes, he is preparing a place for us in the future (which many of us are scared will actually be rather lame and tame). But exciting, exhilarating, and electrifying—right here and right now? Nope. Those aren't the words many of us use when talking about faith, church, worship, or prayer.

"Hey, psst, psst you, yeah you! You want to have a good time tonight? Let's read the Bible!" "Hey, hey you, you looking to be blown away—let's pray!" "Hey, you want the ride of a lifetime? Let's go share our faith in Christ with others!"

When it comes to fascination, we tend to walk away from God instead of walking closer to him. This mindset is a complete shame and a huge mistake because of the incredible promise in the Psalms: *"You make known to me the path of life; you will fill me with joy in your presence, with eternal pleasures at your right hand"* (Ps. 16:11).

We tend to spend all of our time chasing after everything but God when it comes to our desire for fascination. Yet, the promise is that in his presence is overflowing joy, and that out of his right hand are unending, limitless pleasures. God possesses the very things you and I are trying to find everywhere else.

Don't you think that God, the Creator of the cosmos, knows how to get crazy? Don't you think that God, the author of all that we see, can give you all you can handle and more? Don't you think that the Eternal One has the ability to excite everyone? Of course he can. It's what he does best.

Look At That!

You want to be fascinated? The apostle Paul says look at the works of God's hands: *"For since the creation of the world God's invisible qualities—his eternal power and divine nature—have been clearly seen, being understood from what has been made, so that people are without excuse"* (Rom. 1:20).

From the simplest cells to the enormity of the solar system, everything God made is designed to blow us away. And every day, in every moment, we should be fascinated by what we see all around us. That was definitely the case for Job:

> But as for me, I would seek God, and I would place my cause before God; Who does great and unsearchable things, wonders without number. He gives rain on the earth, and sends water on the fields.
> (Job 5:8–10 NASV)

If I said to someone, "My God does great and unsearchable things, he does wonders without number," and they responded, "Really, like what?" I'm not sure I would say, "Oh, you want to know? Well, how about ... rain!"

But Job is serious. He truly felt that rain was one of the great, unsearchable wonders of God.

I'm not sure I shared Job's enthusiasm for rain until I actually learned about all of the fascinating things that have to happen (especially in places like the Middle East) for rain to actually fall to the ground.

I'm not a scientist, but I'll do my best to explain it to you. First, the water has to travel several hundred miles from the sea through the sky. Next, somehow as the water is in the sky, the salt has to be removed from it so it won't kill everything it touches later on. Then the water has to be large enough as it comes out of the clouds so that it doesn't just dissolve or evaporate into thin air, but it can't be too big or else it will crush the very fields it is designed to nourish. And in addition to size, there is the speed factor. The rain has to come down at the perfect speed so that it doesn't rip through the earth and kill everybody.

And that's just part of the process!

Rain? Come on, it's just rain. But oh how amazing and fascinating it really is! Job was right.

In addition to rain, Job could have mentioned a ton of different things. He could have said God does wonders without number like:

The earth's perfect rotation, tilt, and placement from the sun, *or*
The complexities and intricacies of cell biology, *or*
The fact that all the info in our DNA would fill up an entire library, *or*
Astrophysics *or* chemical engineering, *or* nuclear physics, or....

Our God does wonders without number! He is truly fascinating!

Copernicus, Newton, and Einstein did great things, but they more or less just discovered and "unearthed" some of the amazing ways in which God works. The very things that some people think disprove God actually give greater evidence and support for him! Science and religion are not at odds. They help explain and make sense of one another. Science is the manifestation of God's order, might, and power. Whether it's the size of the universe or the intricacies of the human cell, every discovery proves to us that our God is fascinating. He has buried amazing things for us to find, and every time we do we should be filled with awe!

Listen to more of Job's thoughts on this:

He spreads out the northern skies over empty space; he suspends the earth over nothing.

He wraps up the waters in his clouds, yet the clouds do not burst under their weight.

He covers the face of the full moon, spreading his clouds over it.

He marks out the horizon on the face of the waters for a boundary between light and darkness.

The pillars of the heavens quake, aghast at his rebuke.

By his power he churned up the sea…

And these are but the outer fringe of his works; how faint the whisper we hear of him!

Who then can understand the thunder of his power? (Job 26:7–14 NIV)

The northern skies, the horizon line, the sun, moon, and stars, the pillars of heaven, the churning sea—all of those things, things that should absolutely blow our minds, are what Job calls the fringes of God's force! They are merely the strings on the bottom of his jeans! The faintest whisper of his voice! Are you kidding me? The very things that we know so little about, like the sun or the sea—are just an appetizer? That's just God getting warmed up?

God is completely fascinating—who he is and what he has made. You don't have to look anywhere but to him if you want to be left in awe. Anytime you are engaging God's world, exploring God's world, adventuring in God's world, or even just studying God's world—that is God coming through on his promise in Psalm 37:4 to satisfy our deepest desires.

You Are Invited

But more than simply showing us fascinating wonders, our God actually invites us to be a part of his fascinating work. We serve a fascinating God who invites us to do something fascinating with and for him.

In the book of John, Jesus says something rather absurd and hard to believe:

> *Very truly I tell you, whoever believes in me will do the works I have been doing, and they will do even greater things than these, because I am going to the Father. And I will do whatever you ask in my name, so that the Father may be glorified in the Son.* (Jn. 14:12–13 NIV)

"Greater things than these?" Did I just hear you right, Jesus? Your followers will do greater things than you did? You mean greater things than healing broken people? Greater things than illuminating dark places? Greater things than multiplying food or walking on water or raising people from the dead?

Greater things than those? According to Jesus himself, the answer is a resounding yes! That is an incredible promise. More than that, it is an invitation to do and be a part of something truly fascinating. In other words, Jesus is telling us in this passage that we were made for the miraculous. Let that sink in for a minute. The way you have been made is miraculous, but more than that, you were literally made *for* the miraculous.

Typically, though, we read passages like the one in John 14, and we cast it off as being fictitious and fabricated. But what if Jesus was actually telling the truth here? What if he was giving us the power and ability to do the incredible and unthinkable? What if he was promising to blow our minds and leave us and this world in complete awe?

In the book of Ephesians, the apostle Paul says that the same power that raised Jesus from the dead is now in us. It is called the Holy Spirit. The very life, breath, fire, and resurrection power of God himself is in us! Shouldn't that allow, empower, and even compel us to step out in the supernatural?

If you want to be fascinated, read Mark 11:

> *Truly I tell you, if anyone says to this mountain, 'Go, throw yourself into the sea,' and does not doubt in their heart but believes that what they say will happen, it will be done for them.* (Mark 11:23)

Do you realize that, if you are a Christian, you have the ability to move the mountains that cover the earth? Maybe Jesus is referring to mountains like Pike's Peak or Mt. Rushmore, or maybe he's talking about the mountain of guilt that some of your friends are under right now. Or how about the mountain of fear, shame, sexual sin, perfectionism, or doubt that people are struggling to climb? In Christ, through the Spirit, you can throw those mountains into the sea! You can help people overcome and conquer those things. That is utterly fascinating!

Oh no wait, you want to be fascinated? You have to read James 5:

> *Are any of you suffering hardships? You should pray. Are any of you happy? You should sing praises. Are any of you sick? You should call for the elders of the church to come and pray over you, anointing you*

with oil in the name of the Lord. Such a prayer offered in faith will heal the sick, and the Lord will make you well. And if you have committed any sins, you will be forgiven. Confess your sins to each other and pray for each other so that you may be healed. The earnest prayer of a righteous person has great power and produces wonderful results. Elijah was as human as we are, and yet when he prayed earnestly that no rain would fall, none fell for three and a half years! Then, when he prayed again, the sky sent down rain and the earth began to yield its crops. (James 5:13–18 NLT)

Do you realize that you have the ability to help sick people become well? Do you realize you have the ability to help someone experience complete forgiveness and wholeness? Do you realize you have the ability to press into heaven so fervently that you actually affect what happens here on the earth? I'm not sure many of us would describe our prayer life as "fascinating," but why not? That's exactly what it can be and exactly what it is! In prayer, we were talking to the God of the universe and we are promised that we will always have his ear and his heart. That's fascinating. Try it. Live as if God can and actually will answer your prayers, and just wait to see what happens.

You want adventure? Read Mark 6 and the miraculous feeding of the five thousand. In that story, the disciples have had an extremely long day, and right around dinner time, they ask Jesus if they can send everybody away because everyone is getting a little "hangry." It's not a crazy or ridiculous request at all. Then we read this:

But he answered, "You give them something to eat." They said to him, "That would take more than half a year's wages! Are we to go and spend that much on bread and give it to them to eat?" "How many loaves do you have?" he asked. "Go and see." (Mark 6:37–38)

"You give them something to eat!" Wouldn't you have loved to see the look on the disciples faces after Jesus said those words? It is a ridiculous thing to say. Here's what that might sound like today. "Christian, I want you to take care of the homelessness problem in your city. Small group, I want you to figure out how to find a home for every foster child in this state. Church, I want you to help fund and finance every single mother's dreams in the US."

We'd be like, "Jesus, are you smack out of your mind? That would take a crazy amount of resources and tons of time. We'd need millions of dollars, let alone approval and assistance from some of the most important people in the country. It's not doable. It's way bigger than us."

But instead of saying, "Oh yeah, you're right, that was a dumb idea, what was I thinking?" I believe Jesus would ask us the exact same thing he asked the disciples back then: "Well what do you have? How about you get busy using and utilizing the things you do have available and trust that I will take care of the rest. Let's go!" Doing the impossible, the miraculous, and the supernatural is what God does best. He is a God of adventure and awe. A God of miracles and marvels. Trust him. Try him. Join him!

This is the kind of stuff that should fascinate us. This is what we were created for. This is the greatest adventure we could ever go on.

Let me share an example of how I've seen this play out. There was a group of young people out in Southern California called the Circuit Riders. It was a group of incredibly passionate and evangelistic students who were more or less doing revivals on campuses up and down the West Coast.

When they came to Pepperdine, they lit the place up (in a good way, not in the massive wildfire kind of way). They walked into the cafeteria and started teaching people about Jesus, and people listened and responded. They walked through the halls and started praying for healing, and people were healed. They challenged the Christians to live more radically and faithfully, and they did. And it was one of the most fascinating things I have ever seen or been a part of. It was as if Jesus actually meant what he said. And, it's as if I was finally doing what my heart longed for me to do. It was the craziest, most exhilarating adventure I had ever been on, and although that particular revival came to an end, the feeling of being fascinated by God never should.

Come To Me!

People tend to think that God, Jesus, and Christianity as a whole are boring, burdensome, lame, and tame.

Not my God. Not my Jesus.

They are actually the only things that will leave me speechless and amazed. They are the only things that can push me out of my funk and boredom.

In God, through God, because of God, and with God, we can spend our entire lives discovering more about his fascinating world and participating in his fascinating work. Bored? Grab your Bible and read it as an invitation to be blown away, now and for all of eternity. Bored? Go serve someone and see how God fills your cup. Bored? Put on a monkey suit and share your faith. I'll explain that in the next chapter when we talk about devotion.

Drive This Desire Home

To drive this desire home, I challenge you to try one of the following things.

Make A List

Take a few minutes and list all of the things that excite you. Where do you turn for fascination? What are the adventures that you seek? What gets your heart really pumping? Once your list is complete, I want you to go back and see how many of the things on your list are overtly spiritual or Christian. Be honest. Did serving, loving, praying, sharing, or evangelism come up on your list at all? Why or why not? Why do you think fascination must come outside of and apart from your faith?

Be Amazed

Take a look at the world around you. Look at a baby (without creeping out the mom). Look up at the stars. Stand out in the rain. Pick up an old textbook. Dig in the dirt. Discover again, or maybe for the first time, how amazing God's creation is. Spend a few minutes (or hours, or days) being reminded of how great God is based upon the amazing works of his hands.

Take A Look

Read the first few verses of Hebrews 6:

> *Therefore let us move beyond the elementary teachings about Christ and be taken forward to maturity, not laying again the foundation of repentance from acts that lead to death, and of faith in God, instruction about cleansing rites, the laying on of hands, the resurrection of the dead, and eternal judgment. And God permitting, we will do so.* (Heb. 6:1–3)

Now answer the following questions—if "repentance from acts that lead to death," "faith in God," "the resurrection of the dead," and "eternal judgment," are "elementary teachings" in God's eyes, then what are the deeper spiritual truths that God wants to reveal to us? What's the next-level of learning or maturity or revelation? Ask God to take you beyond the basics and into the mind-blowing.

Try It

Put this book down and go outside and share your faith with the very next person you run into. I don't care if it's a random stranger or your mom. Go to a hospital or a nursing home and start praying for and over people. Step out in faith and do something freaky, fascinating, or faith shaking. Watch God use your words and your courage to do something incredible. Adventure awaits, and it starts the moment you take a risk for God.

WHO'S THE GUY IN THE MONKEY SUIT?
DEVOTION

There are certain questions in life that people have asked and debated for centuries. These questions have the ability to pierce the soul and reveal a person's true character. These questions should definitely be asked on a first date or before you ever go into business with someone. These are questions like, "What is your favorite topping on a burger (seriously, that's about all you need to know about someone, isn't it?)? Or how about, "If you could be any Disney character, which one would you be" (again, total game changer, but today's youth have it so easy now that Disney owns everything)? And then there is a question that I have always loved to ask: "What is your favorite movie?"

We have three girls under the age of twelve, so the only movies my wife and I ever get to watch typically involve purple, singing dinosaurs, or cute, fairy princesses (I'm not complaining. I'm just saying.). But when I was super cool and hip, I used to love watching movies like *Braveheart, Gladiator,* and *Remember The Titans* (and if you have not yelled out "FREEEEEDOM," "Are you NOT entertained?," and

"Right side, STRONG SIDE" at some point in this life, then you haven't truly lived).

Our favorite movies all have one major thing in common. Yes, there are different characters and crises. Sure there are different settings and special effects. But all of them, at one level or another, powerfully speak to our next desire, the desire we all have for devotion.

Devotion

There is something deep inside us that comes alive when we see or experience true devotion, whether to the girl, the team, or the cause. We are inspired by those who play with, fight for, and give their whole lives to something. We love those who are willing to lay it all down and give it all up. We cheer for those who have an unwavering focus and an uncanny determination and resolve.

From Katniss Everdeen, to Michael Jordan, to the lovesick couple in the newest Nicholas Sparks novel—we love characters who serve, play, fight, work, and love with their whole hearts. Characters who are willing to go anywhere and do anything. Those who won't give up, who won't let go, and who won't take "no" for an answer. We are drawn to those whose hearts burn with unbridled passion and devotion, those who overcome seemingly insurmountable obstacles to accomplish great things. That's why we watch sports, or go to the movies, or award people with different prizes and honors.

That's why my friend wore a monkey suit.

Okay, let me explain.

One day my ministry interns and I were brainstorming

the best way to promote a new worship service that we were launching at a local college. We talked about handing out flyers, doing a social media campaign, and giving away a ton of free stuff. We all felt pretty good about our commitment to this project until we showed up the next day and saw Jason. Jason was wearing a full, life-sized, super hairy, somewhat creepy monkey suit. And not only was he wearing the suit, but he was running from class-to-class handing out bananas (I say "handing out," but it actually looked more like an all-out attack!). We were all a tad bit confused to say the least. We finally got a chance to talk to monkey-boy and we couldn't help but ask, "What are you doing? I thought we were going to talk with people and hand out some fliers?"

Jason looked straight at us through his black plastic monkey eyes, and said, "Everyone does banners. Nobody does bananas!"

Hard to argue with that.

I learned a profound truth that day—always ask Jason to be your hype man for an event. But more than that, I learned that devotion means doing more than most people are willing to do and going further than most people are willing to go. True, deep, heartfelt devotion is more costly and more risky than we think, but the impact and possibilities are greater than we could even imagine.

As I mentioned before, we see glimpses of deep devotion in different places in our world. The greatest athletes of all time have been totally dedicated and devoted to their respective sports. In football, all-time-great receiver Jerry Rice was so devoted that he was out running laps and doing ladders the day after the 49ers had just won the Super Bowl.

Or take Gabby Douglas. She started gymnastics at the age of three, and for fifteen years she was homeschooled so she could be in the gym eight to ten hours a day.

We see devotion in the arts as well. Actors and actresses spend countless hours memorizing their scripts in the hopes of getting the part. Nature photographers spend innumerable nights out in the wilderness in the hopes of catching the perfect shot.

And yet, most of our lives are lived in stark contrast to that level of dedication. Words like "devoted" or "dedicated" don't immediately come to mind when I think about my average day. Words like "distracted," "disinterested," or even "depleted" seem more appropriate.

I think about sports. At 6' 0" and 175 pounds, I am definitely not what you would call an athletic specimen. And although I wasn't going to make a living playing professional sports, I could throw a decent spiral and could catch almost anything hit to center field. Even though I was experiencing some success in high school sports, I quit every single one of them by the middle of my junior year because I considered them to be too demanding. I threw in the towel because I was being asked to work too hard and give too much. Sorry, Coach Mead and Coach Barker. I should have been more devoted.

I think about school (especially college). I don't know about you, but I didn't exactly run out and buy every book on the suggested reading list. I learned what it would take to get the grade I wanted (which more or less meant cramming and then coasting). I started college as a biology major. I was going to be a dentist, but the introductory classes were way too hard. So I dropped that major and joined all of the athletes in communications. Sorry, professors, athletes, and future dental patients. I should have been more devoted.

I think about relationships. I barely stay in contact with my closest friends from high school or college. Besides the occasional Facebook reminder, I wouldn't even know it's anyone's birthday (and sadly, that's even true when it comes to some of my closest family). When people are standing right in front of me, sharing something important, I tend to be rather distracted by other things, especially my phone! Sorry 1,346 Facebook friends. I should be more devoted.

I tried to learn to play the guitar multiple times, but as soon as my fingers started hurting, I gave that up. There are numerous pieces of workout equipment and exercise videos lying around my house—all collecting dust. And I can't tell you how many times I have committed to eating healthy—but two words have kept me from that every single time: Krispy Kreme!

The list of failures and resignations is pretty long. I could keep going, but I think you get the point (and I think I sound like a big enough loser). But in all honesty, I haven't been fully devoted to anything! And chances are, you can relate.

- We all love the new boyfriend or girlfriend until someone more intriguing or more attractive comes around and starts showing interest.
- We are all super excited about the new car until the first door ding, scratch, or food spill.
- We are all devoted to a certain hobby, job, or class,

as long as it is easy and doesn't require a ton of
extra work.

- We all get pretty excited about the team or the
cause until the team loses or the cause isn't so hip
or popular anymore.

Disinterest, distraction, and diversion are the default
setting now in our society. Don't agree with me, just look
down at your phone. A recent study found that the average
iPhone user touches his or her phone 2,617 times a day.[1]
Each user is on their phone, on average, two and half hours,
over seventy-six sessions every day (that's EVERY user
including your grandma).[2] Let's bring it a bit closer to
home. A study on Millennials put those numbers at twice
that much. 5,000 touches. Five hours per day. Over one-
hundred sessions per day.[3]

You talk about distraction. It's in every
beep/ring/alert/vibration/or notification. But the problem is
that the distraction we experience with our phones is actually seeping into our faith. Think about your relationship to
the Lord for a minute. I imagine that a lot of us are either
stuck in the ritual of religion (I do this or that because
that's what I've always done), or we mindlessly just go
through the motions where we check off certain boxes like
going to church or reading the Bible because that's what
that's what we've been told to do. I mean honestly, in
comparison to how dedicated you are to keeping up with
your IG account, or your fantasy football team, or the
newest Netflix original series, or even just the random
gossip on the internet—how devoted are you to God right
now? Do you offer up 5,000 prayers a day? Are you reading

the Bible five hours a day? Do you participate in over one-hundred different worship sessions?

Probably not.

And at some level that is okay, because that would just be crazy, right?! To give something that much time. Ridiculous. To give something that much energy. Inconceivable. To give something that much devotion.

Oh wait. We already do. You see, our hearts are wired for devotion. It's not a matter of *will* we be devoted to something, it's a matter of *what* we will devote ourselves to.

But my heart aches for more. And I think yours does too. My heart aches to be devoted, to be dedicated, to give myself fully to a cause and a calling that is so much greater than myself and one that actually deserves all of myself. I don't want to be so wishy-washy. I don't want to give up so easily. I don't want to just play the game, or just go through the motions, or for my attention to be so distracted by every alert, or post, or show, or squirrel.

The FOMO Is Real

You all have heard of FOMO—the fear of missing out. Truth be told, because we are so distracted, disjointed, and divided when it comes to our attention and affections, because we aren't truly devoted to that which matters the most, we should be afraid because we are actually missing out. We are missing out on this good, godly, abundant life that God has for us.

You were not meant to live a life that is done half-way or half-heartedly. You were made by a driven, devoted, and dedicated God to live a driven, devoted, and dedicated life.

Pastor Mike Bickle said it this way: "Half-heartedness diminishes our glory as human beings made in the image of God."[4] Half-heartedness, in every area of life, but especially when it comes to our faith, is hurting us so badly. We have been made for more. We have been called to give more.

Listen to how King David said it in Psalm 27:4:

> Here's the one thing I crave from God, the one thing I seek above all else: I want the privilege of living with him every moment in his house, finding the sweet loveliness of his face, filled with awe, delighting in his glory and grace, I want to live my life so close to him that he takes pleasure in my every prayer. (Passion)

Is that the cry of our hearts? Is that the longing of our souls? One thing above all else—God!!!! Until it is, I'm not sure we will ever live in the fullness that God has for us.

Author and pastor John Mark Comer recently rocked my world with his book *The Ruthless Elimination of Hurry*. Something he said in that book stopped me dead in my tracks. John Mark said this: "What you give your attention to is the person you become.... In the end, your life is no more than the sum of what you gave your attention to."[5]

Stop and think about that for a minute. Your life is more or less the sum of the things you spent the most time doing or watching or consuming. Good news for those who read the Bible all day, serve every extra second they get, and sing praise songs in their sleep. Bad news for everybody else in the world whose attention is so divided and who spend ridiculous amounts of time scrolling, swiping, or binge-watching.

So, if we are what we give our attention or devotion to,

what if we aren't really paying attention to or devoted to anything? What if we aren't actually committed to anyone? If our attention and devotion isn't directed at anything of significance or worth or value, what does that say about us?

Where To Start

The only way we grow in our dedication and devotion to the Lord is to be overwhelmed by his dedication and devotion to us. You can't start this process by just mustering up more devotion or more passion for God. It might work for a few minutes, but then you will fall back into the world of distraction. You have to focus your eyes, heart, and mind on the devotion that our great God has for us. Then—and only then—will you be compelled to give him your all. Because that's exactly what he did for you.

Let me explain why.

Throughout all of Scripture, God's devotion never waivers. His passion never wanes. His dedication is never in doubt, even when his people continue to do the dumbest things. But nowhere is that more evident than at the cross.

As I stare at the cross, I hear God saying so many things. I hear him telling me he loves me (what else would motivate someone to do that?). I hear him telling me how horrible the consequences of my selfishness and sin really are (why not choose to die in a way that was more pain free or even painless?). I hear him telling me how justice, mercy, grace, and wrath can all come together in a singular moment (Jesus truly is the only one who can hold all things together, even seemingly contradictory things). But I also hear something else. I hear God telling me that he's "All in!"

The Bible says in John 15:13 that there is no greater expression of devotion, dedication, focus, and commitment than the cross. There is no greater love than a man laying down his life so that his friends—you and I— would finally be able to start living ours. Hanging on the cross, Jesus more or less says, "This is how serious I am. This is how committed I am. This is what matters to me. This is how loyal and dedicated I am." Everything Jesus said with his lips before the cross, he sealed with his blood on the cross!

And you have been made in the image of this God. You have been made to reflect these same qualities. God has hard-wired you to model and to make known qualities and characteristics like dedication, devotion, single-mindedness, and loyalty. They run through your DNA. They are an inseparable part of who you are.

And oh, how badly this world—a world plagued by half-heartedness, mediocrity, divided hearts, short attention spans, and boredom—needs to see and experience those things from us. Devotion and dedication are things the unbelieving world longs to see and experience, and Christians have been tasked to show them just that.

Leftovers

Let me ask you a simple question: do you like leftovers? Although some things definitely aren't as good the following day (or week), I love opening the fridge and seeing some leftovers. "Oh, sweet heavens! I don't have to think or work very hard right now! I can just heat this stuff up and get my feast on! Thank you, God, for leftovers!"

But, in life there is a very different type of leftovers.

There is the attention kind. The commitment kind. The energy kind.

When Becca and I are struggling in our marriage, we can almost always point to the fact that we haven't been giving one another our first, best, or our complete selves. We have grown lazy and lackadaisical in our love. We call that our "leftovers." And if you are not careful, you can end up giving everyone, including your family, your church, or your God— your leftovers.

Although I'm sure God loves some cold pizza (it was probably what he ate on the seventh day when he rested), I don't think he is a very big fan of life leftovers. He never gives us his. He never gives us his scraps or his bits and pieces. In return, he asks that we never give him ours either.

All Of It??!!

I grew up in the Sandia Mountains just outside of Albuquerque, New Mexico. One of my chores was to stack firewood on my parent's front porch. I can remember the very first time I was asked to do this particular task. My dad bought me a cool, lumberjack-looking plaid shirt. I got to wear real work gloves and a pair of my dad's old work boots. I was pretty excited to say the least. I remember thinking, "I am all that is man. I stack wood. I keep house warm!"

Then my dad took me out to the wood pile, and everything changed. There in front of me stood what looked like a demolished Red Wood Forest, an enormous pile of logs that extended seven-miles-wide and five-miles-high (it barely filled up our driveway but we had a really BIG driveway). After breaking out of my stupor, I turned to my dad and said, "You want me to stack all of it?"

He nonchalantly turned to me and said, "Yes, son. ALL of it!"

And then he walked back into the house and probably fell asleep on the couch!

All of it. That is what our Father gave to us and is what he wants from us. That is what our Father deserves from us. That is what our Father is inviting us into—all of it!

To prove it, we don't need to look any further than Jesus' words in Mark 12. Several times Jesus was asked what the single greatest command in all the Law was. Do you remember what he said? *"Love the Lord your God with ALL your heart, ALL your soul, ALL your mind, and ALL your strength"* (Mark 12:30 NLT, emphasis mine).

I wish that I could just chalk this verse up as Jesus exaggerating or saying things to get a response from the crowd. But that's just not true. He always meant what he said, and he always said what he meant.

God wants ALL of us. He wants us to be fully devoted and completely dedicated to him! He wants all of our hearts, all of our minds, all of our energy, and all of our soul. He wants complete loyalty, not some cold leftovers. In other words, Jesus was telling us to have a magnificent obsession with God. To have this preoccupation with our Heavenly Father. To default to loving, serving, worshipping, thinking about, and praying to the Lord all day, everyday. It's as if Jesus was challenging us to engage with God the way we engage our phones.

I always have it on me. I'm always checking in to see what's going on. I'm always connected and touching base. I just can't live without it and start freaking out when I can't find it.

But what compels us to that level of devotion is a deeper understanding of the Father's devotion. God doesn't hold anything back. God doesn't go halfway or do things to a certain point. God doesn't give up when things get too tough or demanding. God doesn't quit or check out because he's tired. God doesn't only show up or serve us on Sundays.

So why am I?   Why are you? Life, especially life in Christ, is not designed to be done half-heartedly.

Devotion and loyalty are all-or-nothing propositions. A spouse who is 85 percent faithful isn't faithful or loyal at all. There is no such thing as part-time or semi- loyalty. You are either all in, or you are not in at all.

Not A Christian Anymore

I am saddened whenever I hear young people tell me that they have given up on God and aren't going to follow Christ any longer. I always try to follow up by asking what exactly they mean by that statement. Typically they proceed to tell me that they are giving up on a rather stale set of religious practices that are nothing more than a list of do's and don'ts, a list of behaviors they have been told to perform so they can please God (and/or their parents and/or their pastor). They are telling me they want to give up on a co-curricular activity where you praise God on Sundays and worship him in church settings, but then live your life however you want the rest of the week and worship every-thing else once church is over. A lifestyle where you compartmentalize your Christianity and only do the "Jesus thing" when it is easy, convenient, or beneficial—which isn't very often and ends up looking and feeling incredibly hypocritical.

They are leaving a relationship with God that is an odd combination of some Biblical truths, some pop/positive psychology, some self-help material, some American dream, and a few Bible apps.

Well, that's not Christianity.

If you want to give up on that, then go ahead. I would give up on empty, habitual, half-hearted, lifeless, phony, insincere, confusing, busy work-type religious practices as well.

But you can't in good conscience give up on something you have never actually tried! Before you stop being a Christian, how about you honestly and wholeheartedly try to be one first? How about you give God everything, ALL of you, and then see what happens?

If I told you I was giving up on gymnastics, you would probably want to know how long I had been a gymnast. What if I said, "Well, I never actually did gymnastics. I rolled around on the floor a few times, and I tried to do a headstand once, but gymnastics wasn't ever really my thing. So I'm done with it, and I can't believe others would waste their time with that stuff!!!"

See the problem? I'm giving up on, quitting, and badmouthing something I was never actually committed to. In that scenario, I would only be quitting my weak, halfhearted, embarrassing attempts at gymnastics. I wouldn't be giving up on the real thing. I wonder if that same dynamic applies to faith.

"All or nothing!" is how God made us to live. You were created by a passionate, whole, devoted, zealous God to live a passionate, whole, devoted, and zealous life. Until you do, you won't ever be fully alive. And before we give up on God, how about we actually completely dedicate ourselves to God? A lot of folks are more or less just "playing church," just going through the motions and sitting on the sidelines when it comes to faith.

And I get it.

- We are afraid of what it will cost if we decide to go all in for God.
- We are worried what others will say if we crank up our commitment level to Christ.
- We are nervous that we won't like what we will find or that we will be disappointed with what we will get in return when we totally dedicate ourselves to serving others.
- We doubt that God will actually show up or come through on his promises if we truly seek him first.
- We assume we won't be able to get everything done if we actually take a Sabbath and just rest in God.

It's easier to hedge your bet, to only go halfway. It's easier to play it safe (or just play the game) and not really give it your all. But that hesitation and reluctance is hurting us at so many levels!

Give All, Get All

Why would God say what he did in Mark 12? Why would God command us to love him with all that we are and all that we have? Is he insecure? Does he need more friends or affirmation or praise? Or is he just assigning us a ton of busy work?

Absolutely not. His insistence on our wholehearted devotion to him is for our benefit not his. Loving God with all of our hearts is the only way to experience the fullness of what it means to be alive. You might think that a passionate desire for God is our gift to him, when it is actually his gift to us! We were made to give God all of ourselves because when we do, we will actually find ourselves.

It's weird how it happens, but it does. I begin to have more passion for everything else in life only as I grow in my passion for the Lord.

- I begin to love my wife more when I fall more in love with God.
- I begin to love my friends and family more when I fall more in love with God.
- I begin to love snowboarding, golf, and food more when I fall more in love with God! I always love food, but still, God makes it so much better.

As my devotion to God increases so does my capacity to devote myself to other things.

But the opposite is not true. Not in the least. When anything other than God becomes the sole object of my affection, when anything other than the Lord becomes what

I live and die for, when anything besides Christ becomes that which I devote my life to—it will actually end up ripping life away from me. That's true for all of us.

- Ask the guy who completely lost his friends because he was so obsessed with his hobbies or his grades.
- Ask the gal who destroyed her mind and body because she was so committed to looking a certain way and maintaining a certain body image.
- Ask the young executives who lost their minds because they were so dedicated to making more money or climbing the corporate ladder.

If we pursue anything else with the fervor and passion that we have been created to give to God, and God alone, it will end up taking everything from us. And it can happen quickly without you even knowing it.

- That pursuit of happiness you are on, the one where you buy everything you want, even if you can't afford it, is actually destroying the other areas of your life. Credit card debt and being enslaved to monthly payments is a huge black cloud that is always over your head, and it actually dictates and determines your next step, even if you don't realize it.
- That fun, flirtatious relationship you have with your co-worker, the one that seems so harmless and innocent? That relationship is easily going to turn into an all out extramarital affair and even at

this point it is slowly (or not so slowly) taking over every area of your life. It's all you can think about, especially when you should be thinking about something (or someone) else.

- Those negative things you say about yourself and the lies you have come to believe about yourself? Those thoughts and lies almost always lead to cutting, pornography, or drug and alcohol abuse because those negative thoughts and feelings are all-consuming. Those thoughts aren't just a small part of your life. They are truly seeping into and affecting all of your life. And you are living a very guarded, shielded, defensive, and unhealthy life as a result.

When God asks us to give him our all, he is not asking us to do something ridiculous. It's not as if he is asking anything more than that top-notch education, that new corporate job, that hobby, or even that phone of yours is asking of you. They all ask (if not demand) your all. More, more, more and gimme, gimme, gimme says the new app or the new project or the new fling. In telling us to love him with all of ourselves, God is telling us where our devotion and dedication should lie and where it should be focused. We are going to spend our time and dedicate our lives to something (even if that's the black hole of social media or social comparison). God is inviting us to focus our time and attention on him.

Look No Further

Living a life that is full of devotion to the Lord is the way we experience the fullness, abundance, and best in this life. The Bible is full of examples of men and women who prove this to us.

Think of the twelve disciples. They dropped everything—the nets, the jobs, the remotes, the mirror, the books, the iStuff, their hopes and dreams—and they give it their all. When they did, they ended up living incredible lives that changed the world forever. Bringing hope, healing, and the promise of heaven was a far cry from catching a few fish every now and again. They gave their devotion and dedication to something more eternal.

I think of the apostle Paul. He gave up a brilliant career as a Bible scholar with incredible financial advantages. He gave up a position of power and prestige, and instead he sacrificed and suffered for the Lord. But in return, he ended up bringing salvation to people like you and me. Being a big deal during his day was one thing, but being a big deal still to this day? He gave his devotion and dedication to something more important.

Or I think of Mary of Bethany in Matthew 26 as she took her most prized possession, a jar of the finest perfume of the day, something that was most likely worth up to $10,000, and she lavishly poured it over Jesus' feet. Tears were flowing down her face. Dirt was all over her hands. But she didn't count the cost or weigh the options. She viewed all of her life in light of this one man. He wasn't just a part of her life. He was the very essence of her life. She was willing to give him anything and everything. And in return, her name and her story have become the standard and epitome of love and devotion.

We are fascinated by stories like these because that is how we were made to live.

Devotion

Imagine a life that is consumed with, for, and by God. Imagine a Christian who doesn't just give God his or her leftovers but who gives him his or her very best. Imagine what it would look like (or feel like) if we didn't give God a small part of our lives, but instead gave him our entire lives. Imagine truly seeking God first and trusting that he will provide everything else and fill in all of the gaps. Imagine praising God louder on Monday mornings in the classroom or boardroom than you do on Sundays in the sanctuary. Imagine having the Gospel be the lens by which you see everything and everyone and the means by which you make every decision. Imagine giving away or spending just as much money on others as you do yourself. Imagine a heart that is compelled to take action at the sight of injustice and inequality. Imagine giving it *all* to your Father.

We have been called to do far more than imagine all of that.

We have been called to live like that.

We have been called, in a world that is so fragmented and distracted, a world whose hearts and affections are so disjointed and misplaced, to live wholly (and holy) dedicated lives. Sure, the movies are full of great examples of that type of commitment and devotion. But the same should be said of our churches and homes and lives.

When we give ourselves fully to God, I believe we will experience, encounter, and enjoy God in ways that are far greater than anything we can even imagine, which is perfect because that just happens to be our next desire.

Drive This Desire Home

To drive this desire home, I challenge you to try one of the following things.

Focus

Focus more on what God has done for you and less on what you need to do for him.

I know this sounds counterproductive, especially in a chapter that's all about living a more zealous life for Jesus. But the first thing you have to do, doesn't require you to do anything. Marveling at God's devotion *to us* is the first step in becoming more devoted *to him*. It's not about working harder. Most people have it backwards. It's not about doing more. It's not about loading up your religious plate with lots of good things. It's about enjoying the fact that God enjoys you! Let that sink in for a second. The apostle John wrote, *"We love because he first loved us"* (1 Jn. 4:19 NIV).

Our love and devotion are rooted and grounded in his love and devotion. One is utterly dependent upon the other. So ...

- Don't get frustrated by *your* lack of devotion to him. Reflect on *his* unending devotion to you.

- Don't beat yourself up because you lose your focus. Be overwhelmed by that fact that Jesus never did.
- Don't assume or act as if you have to prove anything. Stand in awe that Jesus proved and paid it all!

The apostle Paul wrote, *"For the love of Christ compels us"* (2 Cor. 5:14 NIV). Paul's radical devotion to Christ all started because he grasped Christ's radical devotion to him! And all of us will be compelled to love God when we are overwhelmed by his love for us. We will have a stronger passion for Christ when we get a deeper understanding of his passion for us.

A lot of people view God as a distant deity, a cosmic cop, or an angry arbitrator. I can guarantee that you will have far less passion for God if and when you view him as the judge who is trying to punish you for something versus a loving father who rejoices over you with singing.

This week, spend some time reading, reflecting on, and actually enjoying the love and promises of God. Read the Bible in such a way where you insert your name in the blanks, where you trust and believe that God is talking about you when he declares his love and devotion. Take the Word out of the hypothetical or theoretical level and apply it directly to your life and situation. That's how God wrote it, and that's how God wants you to read it.

Do you see, read, and study the Bible as a book that describes what you have to do for God? Or do you see, read, and study the Bible as a book that describes what God has already done for you? Be honest—because the way you answer that question has the power to change everything. It's all about your focus.

Fast

Forego food so that you can feast on Jesus.

I don't know about you, but I love food. From cheap fast food meals, to four-course meals at high-end restaurants, I can eat with the best of them. So when Jesus asks me to give him my all, he couldn't possibly mean my desire for food, could he?

Fasting has become a lost art. That is a shame because it is one of the most powerful ways to increase your passion for and awareness of the Lord. As we fast from food, as we refrain from eating a meal or two or ten, we seek to feast on Jesus.

The hope and the goal in fasting is for God to become enjoyable and more necessary than the meal we are about to eat. The hope and goal for us as believers is to delight more in God than in our taste buds. The hope and goal for us is to serve and savor God more than we do our own appetites.

I suggest fasting for an entire day this week—so that means you give up three meals in a row and only drink water or juice during that time. The hope is that during that time you will experience God's worth, beauty, and fellowship more than you ever have. During those meal times, when those hunger pains come, read, pray, serve, worship, rest, and listen. Zero in on God, and make him your top priority.

For some of you, success will mean just getting through the day. That's fine. My hope, though, is that you won't just get through it, but that you will truly be blessed by it. Fasting is a way to develop our devotion muscles and to sacrifice something for the Lord.

If you are not willing to give up a few meals for Jesus, then chances are you are going to struggle giving him your all.

Forgive

Let go of the pain and shame you are holding onto so God can fill your hands with something better.

It is truly amazing how a wound, a negative experience, or a bad memory from the past can totally dictate, determine, and drive our future. Something that happened years ago, whether at home, at school, in the bedroom, or even in the boardroom, still follows us around today as if it just happened yesterday.

Most of us have been hurt, abused, disappointed, or let down by someone at some point in our lives. It could have been a parent, a friend, a lover, a coach, a mentor, or a pastor. Their sinfulness came out in a way that scarred you. From abuse to neglect, from letting you down to letting you go—people have the power and ability to hurt us.

But here's the hard truth about all of that. It is going to be extremely hard, if not impossible, to give God your all when you are still holding on to all of that hurt. It is going to be hard, if not impossible, to open your hands and receive what God has planned for you when your hands are clenched tightly around someone else's neck. Before you can give your all to God, you truly have to forgive the people in your life that have hurt or disappointed you the most.

That's why the word "give" is in the word "forgive." When you forgive someone you are truly giving something away and giving something up. When you forgive another, you are giving up your anger, your frustration, your pain, your disappointment, your lawsuit, your vendetta, etc. Forgiving others is a huge step in giving God your all.

But in addition to forgiving others, many of us need to forgive ourselves. It's one thing to think about the things that have (or have not) been done to us. It's another to think about the things that we have done to ourselves (and/or to others). Forgiving ourselves, and giving God our mistakes, regrets, and pain is no easy task. But it is truly the first step in finding satisfaction to your desire for devotion. You can't give God your whole, complete self when you hate yourself or keep beating yourself up.

God is not simply asking for you to surrender those parts of your life that are presentable and that you are pleased with. He is asking for all of it. Coming to terms with the fact that you are an imperfect sinner, and then forgiving yourself for however that sin manifested itself in the past (or in the present), is critical if you want to start living a God-centric, all-in life. Hatred, hurt, and a hard heart have a way of weighing us down and keeping us from the life God intended. Let those things go and start living fully for God.

---

1. Julia Naftulin, "Research Shows We Touch Our Cell Phones 2,617 Times per Day." Business Insider Australia. Business Insider Australia, July 13, 2016. https://www.businessinsider.com.au/dscout-research-people-touch-cell-phones-2617-times-a-day-2016-7.

2. Michael Winnick and Robert Zolna. "Putting a Finger on Our Phone Obsession." Resources for remote, qualitative and in-context research, https://blog.dscout.com/mobile-touches.

3. Kari Paul, "Millennials Waste Five Hours a Day Doing This One Thing." New York Post. New York Post, July 26, 2017. https://nypost.com/2017/05/18/millennials-waste-five-hours-a-day-doing-this-one-thing/.

4. Mike Bickle and Deborah Hiebert, *The Seven Longings of the Human Heart*, (Kansas City, MO: Forerunner Books, 2006).

5. John Mark Comer and John Ortberg. *The Ruthless Elimination of Hurry: Staying Emotionally Healthy and Spiritually Alive in Our Current Chaos*, (Colorado Springs: WaterBrook, 2019).

I > YOU

GREATNESS

A few years ago, Lady Gaga came out with a song named "Applause." It's appropriately titled because it goes something like this: "I live for the applause, applause, applause, I live for the applause, plause, I live for the applause, plause...." I'd keep going, but I think you get the idea.

Although that little tune isn't terribly complicated or creative, it is very catchy. And more than that, it perfectly describes our next desire, one that I resonate with more than all the rest.

The desire for greatness.

I am what people would call "a little competitive." To put it plainly, I hate losing with every fiber of my being. From board games to the board room, I want to be the best!

When I was a kid, I cried every single time I struck out in baseball (which was more than I would like to admit). As a child, I would throw video game controllers across the room when my perfect Madden season was about to come to an end. One time, I spanked myself with a ping-pong paddle so profusely (after losing a match to my best friend at the time) that I broke the paddle and nearly ruined the friendship.

And then there is Stacker. Stacker was an arcade game that came out when I was in college that nearly cost me my salvation. I seriously came close to spending time behind bars because of that stupid game,(okay, it never got *that* bad, but let's just say after I lost for the tenth time in a row, you would have never guessed I was a pastor, or even a Christian).

You see, I want to win—at everything. I want to be the best—in every situation. Not only that, but I want other people to see *and know* that I'm the best.

Take my high school letterman jacket as an example. That jacket was basically an overpriced leather coat with pompous and pretentious patches all over it, from sports awards to student government letters. I even had my last name and presidential title plastered all over the back, just in case you didn't know either of those two things. Let's just say I was pretty full of myself back then, and like Lady Gaga, I definitely lived for the applause!

All of the desires that we have discussed up until this point resonate deep in my heart. But more than all of the others, I am driven by a desire for greatness. This is the desire to be the champ, to be crowned the king, and to be carried out of the room or off the field on people's shoulders all of whom are chanting your name.

"Thomas, Thomas, Thomas!"

Go ahead, join in. I don't mind!

This desire probably burns deep inside of your heart too. This is the desire you have to not only play the game, but to crush your opponent while you are at it. This is the desire you have to not only learn a new skill, but to master the new skill and instantly be the best at it. This is the desire you have to not only get a good grade, but to get the highest grade in the class and possibly in the history of the school. This is the desire you have to not only decorate your room, but decorate it in such a way where all your friends post pictures of it on Pintrest and then beg you to come and redecorate their rooms! This is the desire you have to be esteemed and envied by others.

Like Lady Gaga said, this desire is all about the applause!

And even if we don't sing the song or wear letter jackets, we all love to be praised.

Whether its championship trophies, advanced degrees, pay raises, or just more followers on twitter, we all want to be great. We all want to be the big cheese, the big kahuna, or just a big deal. And if you doubt that you are driven by this particular desire, just wait until the applause ends or until people start applauding another. Wait until someone else gets the credit, the job, the praise, or the promotion that you wanted or deserved. Wait until the school, the company, the coach, or the girl thinks there is someone greater than you. Suddenly you will see and feel just how deep this desire truly goes.

But why? Why do we feel this way? Why are we driven by a desire for greatness?

The answer is found on nearly every page of the Bible.

The Greatness of God

We don't have to look very far to see where this desire originates. It's found in multiple places throughout the Old Testament, for example:

> *For great is the Lord and most worthy of praise; he is to be feared above all gods. For all the gods of the nations are idols, but the Lord made the heavens. Splendor and majesty are before him; strength and joy are in his dwelling place.* (1 Chron. 16:25–27 NIV)

We read this in the psalms:

> *Come, let us sing for joy to the Lord; let us shout aloud to the Rock of our salvation. Let us come before him with thanksgiving and extol him with music and song. For the Lord is the great God, the great King above all gods. In his hand are the depths of the earth, and the mountain peaks belong to him. The sea is his, for he made it, and his hands formed the dry land.* (Ps. 95:1–5 NIV)

- You want to be great because God is great.
- You want to be powerful because God is powerful.
- You want to be praised because God is worthy to be praised.

From calling the galaxy into existence at the beginning of time, to calling out the stars last night; from parting the Red Sea, to walking on the Galilean Sea; from being the author or life to the one who defeated death, our God is truly a great and awesome God.

And *you* have been made in *his* image. You have been

created out of that stock. Greatness runs through your veins because God's Spirit and likeness run through your veins. It's not wrong to want to be great. It's actually what you were created for!

The Dark Side

But as is the case with all of the desires, there is a very dark side to our desire for greatness (and no, I'm not doing my best Darth Vader impersonation right now, but feel free to).

This desire can drive us to do some really ugly things. From thinking too highly of ourselves, to arrogantly looking down on others—if we are not careful, our desire for greatness can destroy us and the people around us. Just ask the megachurch pastor who gave into sexual temptation. Just ask the super star athlete who gave into performance-enhancing drugs. Just ask the politician who gave into ... well, take your pick. Your desire for greatness can get you into a lot of trouble.

Listen to how C. S. Lewis put it: "A proud man is always looking down on things and people, and of course, as long as you are looking down, you cannot see the great thing that is above you."[1]

Because we look down on others (or even just down at our phones all day long), we miss the great thing that is above us, not to mention all the amazing things all around us. We all want to be great, but we end up going about it completely wrong.

Most people assume they will be great when they win a competition or get a trophy. Most people assume they will be great when they get a certain number of likes or a certain job title. Most people assume they will be great when they make six digits a year or can purchase the American Dream as seen on TV. Those things can make you arrogant, narcissistic, or egotistical. But they can't make you great. At least not in God's eyes.

We assume what makes us great is our superiority *over* others. We think that what makes us great is the fact that we are more accomplished *than* others. We believe that what makes us great is our ability to stand out *from* others. We live as if the goal is to be applauded *by* others.

But according to the great God of the universe, true greatness has nothing to do with being superior to, standing out from, or shining brighter than others.

It actually has everything to do with serving others.

Let's Give Thomas A Huge Round of Applause!!!!

When it comes to satisfying our desire for greatness in a godly way, Lady Gaga's words still apply. We are called (and created) to live for the applause. The question is *whose* applause?

True greatness is only achieved as we seek and receive the eternal applause of heaven.

Being applauded is one thing. Being applauded by the appropriate audience is another.

Take for example the applause one basketball player received at the end of the big game. He made a last-second, game-winning shot and a huge portion of the crowd went absolutely crazy. Problem was that he made the shot at the wrong end of the court and ended up scoring for the opposing team. Sure there was great applause, but it definitely wasn't the kind he was seeking.

The same is often true for us. We seek the applause of the world, but that's the wrong type of applause and not what we should be striving for. The applause of the world is relatively easy to get and extremely easy to lose. What impresses the masses is fickle and rather fleeting. Think about how quickly we forget about those we once applauded (or why we were even applauding them in the first place). We tend to move on pretty quickly, don't we? Who won the Super Bowl two years ago? Who had the Billboard's top song last year? Who starred in Hollywood's biggest film three years ago?

Here today, gone tomorrow. Applauded today. Forgotten tomorrow.

There is a reason the saying is, "Fifteen minutes of fame." Ask any "one hit wonder," child TV star, or injured athlete. That's about as long as it lasts. Fifteen minutes.

My letterman jacket is an example. No one remembers (or even cares about) what I did back in high school. Although I gave myself wholeheartedly to those endeavors, and although a few people applauded me at the time, it all ended rather abruptly at graduation. In fact, I think I got more boos than applause for all of that hard work (it was well-deserved since I was a real punk).

If you want to be great—truly great—in a way that matters and in a way that lasts, then you need to seek the applause of the Creator not the crowd. If you want to be truly great, then you need to seek the applause of your Maker, and not the masses. If you want to be truly great, then you have to seek the applause of heaven and not the applause of those on the earth. Unlike the applause of this world, which only lasts for fifteen minutes at the most, the applause of heaven will echo for all of eternity.

But what makes heaven applaud? What causes God to rise from his throne and give you a standing ovation?

I'm glad I asked.

For Real?!

I want to show you a passage that completely rocked my world a few years ago. It's found in Luke 22:

> *A dispute also arose among (the disciples) as to which of them was considered to be greatest. Jesus said to them, "The kings of the Gentiles lord it over them; and those who exercise authority over them call themselves Benefactors. But you are not to be like that. Instead, the greatest among you should be like the youngest, and the one who rules like the one who serves. For who is greater, the one who is at the table or the one who serves? Is it not the one who is at the table? But I am among you as one who serves.* (Luke 22:24–27 NIV)

In a group of thirteen guys, I imagine there were a lot of disputes like the one we read about here. In Luke 22, the disciples are debating, and clearly disagreeing over, who was the greatest. If you've ever had the pleasure of listening to a bunch of guys argue about which superstar athlete is the greatest of all time, then you know exactly what this dispute sounded like.

In the middle of their fiery fellowship, Jesus walked up. Given the nature of their conversation, you would expect a stiff rebuke from the Lord, wouldn't you? I would think he might say, "How dare you ask such a thing. How dare you worry about greatness or positions of influence. Have you not heard a single thing that I've been saying to you the last few years? Greatness? Greatness! How foolish and ridiculous of you!"

But that's not what happens at all. There is no rebuke. There is no reprimand. There isn't even a mention of irritation on Jesus' part. Jesus doesn't get mad at the disciples for wanting to be great. He actually affirms their desire. "Oh, you want to be great, do you? Well, let me tell you exactly what that means." Jesus says, *"The greatest among you will be your servant. For those who exalt themselves will be humbled, and those who humble themselves will be exalted"* (Matt. 23:11–12 NIV).

Jesus doesn't denounce the disciples' desire for greatness or deplore them for having it, he actually tells them how to achieve it.

You've already heard me talk about stacking wood for my dad when I was a kid. On one occasion, I remember being asked to take this huge pile of wood that had been delivered in our driveway and move it to the front porch. So I took the wood and randomly threw it into a "pile" onto the porch.

"Boom," I yelled in triumph. Well, out walked my dad to check my progress.

He said, "You call that stacking? That's not stacking! Give me those gloves!"

He then proceeded to stack the wood in a way that would have impressed a mechanical engineer. He put three pieces one way, then three different pieces the opposite way, then another three pieces the original way. In that moment, I realized you needed an advanced degree to stack wood.

After a few minutes, my dad turned to me and said, "That is stacked. Boom."

And I can't help but wonder if Jesus wasn't saying something similar to the disciples as it pertains to their desire for greatness: "You call that greatness? Accumulation, accomplishments, and the applause of the world? Really? That's not greatness. It's not about power or position or prestige. If you want to be great, truly great, great like God, then you are going to have to become the servant of all" (and I bet he said "Boom" right afterward just for good measure).

This has to be one of the most difficult things Jesus ever said. Greatness comes not when you triumph over others or accomplish more than others, but when you serve others! That's what makes heaven stand up and applaud.

And not just any old act of service. Jesus said the servant "of all." Literally the "slave of all." That means serving people you don't know. Or worse, people you don't like. That means serving people who can't pay you back or who will actually take, demand, and ask for more from you. Servant of all means servant of children, the poor, the marginalized, the sick, the imprisoned, Patriots fans (sorry, I had to), or those on the opposite end of the political spectrum as well as those on the other side of the border or tracks. Yes, the servant of *all*.

And Jesus didn't just talk the talk. He walked the walk. That's what makes him so great. Look at how the apostle John describes it:

Before the Passover celebration, Jesus knew that his hour had come to leave this world and return to his Father. He had loved his disciples during his ministry on earth, and now he loved them to the very end. It was time for supper, and the devil had already prompted Judas, son of Simon Iscariot, to betray Jesus. Jesus knew that the Father had given him authority over everything and that he had come from God and would return to God. So he got up from the table, took off his robe, wrapped a towel around his waist, and poured water into a basin. Then he began to wash the disciples' feet, drying them with the towel he had around him. (Jn. 13:1–5 NLT)

The text tells us that in this particular situation, Jesus had authority over everything. In that moment, Jesus could do anything he wanted. Nothing was impossible for him. Nothing was out of reach. Nothing was beyond his ability.

Imagine that.

Imagine you have unlimited resources. Imagine you have the ability to snap your fingers and get anything you want. Imagine you have the strength and authority to accomplish anything your heart desires. Imagine everyone and everything answers to you and has to cater to your every need. When you stop drooling over what that might look or feel like, take a minute to think about what you would actually do.

Would you try to make a name for yourself? Would you do everything you can to enjoy or pamper yourself? Would you hold a press conference to boast or brag about yourself? Would you wow the crowds or live a life of comfort or convenience?

Although we will probably never find ourselves in a situation like that, Jesus did. And at that very moment, when he was truly at his greatest, he picked up a towel and washed twelve pairs of disgusting feet, one of which belonged to the disciple who would ultimately betray him. I highly doubt that many of us would have done the same thing if we were put in that exact same situation. It would be like after Aladdin realized what he had in the lamp with the genie, he wished for a basin of water and a towel so he could wash Jafar's feet.

Give me wealth. Give me power. Give me greatness. Give me Princess Jasmine. Don't give me a menial task to do for undeserving people. No way!

Yet Jesus says (and more importantly shows) that greatness isn't standing on a podium, holding a trophy, or bragging about how much better you are than everybody else. Greatness is about getting on your knees, holding a towel, and serving everybody else.

What makes God so great, and what will ultimately help us satisfy our desire to be the same, is our willingness to humble ourselves and put others' needs above our own. We will be great when we serve and minister to others like God does. Because that's exactly what God does, at least according to Luke:

> Be dressed ready for service and keep your lamps burning, like servants waiting for their master to return from a wedding banquet, so that when he comes and knocks they can immediately open the door for him. It will be good for those servants whose master finds them watching when he comes. Truly I tell you, he will dress himself to serve, he will have them recline at the table and he will come and wait on them (Luke 12:35–37 NIV).

If that passage didn't kick you in the gut or slap you in the face, you need to read it again. Are you kidding me? The master will serve the servants? The great God of the universe who stands above all other gods—will wait on us? That doesn't even make sense. Servants serve and lord's lounge.

Not in God's house.

God's sovereignty isn't the only thing that makes him great, although that is truly incredible. God's strength isn't the only thing that makes him great, although if I were you, I wouldn't mess with him. God's supremacy over all other gods isn't the only thing that makes him great, although no other god comes close to our God. What makes God great is his willingness and desire to serve.

And Jesus says that if we want to be great, then the same needs to be true for us as well.

There is a reason we forget about the vast majority of people out there. It's the same reason the world has never forgotten about Jesus—one type of greatness is fleeting but the other lasts forever.

Where Are The Great Men?

So what does this mean for us? How do we follow the example of Jesus? What does it mean to be great in God's eyes?

I want to talk specifically to the guys for a second. Ladies keep reading, but dudes please pay extra close attention. There is a real shortage of great men in the world today. There are a lot of fake men. There are a lot of immature men. There are a lot of distracted men. There are a lot of apathetic men. But truly great men? Truly godly men? They are in short supply—especially when you define greatness in the way Jesus did.

Guys, my prayer is that each and every one of you would assume the posture of Jesus as seen in John 13. Humble yourself and serve the people around you. I want to challenge you to take this whole foot-washing thing and apply it to your life by doing the following three things.

1) Speak Truth To/Over Your Friends And Family

Several authors believe that in the Garden of Eden, Adam's great sin was that of silence. When Eve was being tempted, when she was being enticed by empty promises and a distorted version of the truth—Adam didn't say a word. He refused to speak up or speak out, and it ended up costing them everything.

Sadly, I think the same is true for a lot of men today. Too many of us refuse to speak the truth over our friends and families. For one, we don't know the truth. We aren't dedicated to the Word like we should so when certain situations come up, we don't know what to say because we don't know what the Bible says. Men, the words that will help you get through the ups and downs (and even the sideways of this life), the words you need to help others navigate difficult situations, and the words that will bring joy and peace and conviction into the lives of those you love are all found in God's Word. We need to speak truth, God's truth, to/over others.

A lot of men remain silent because they are afraid someone will ask them a question they don't know the answer to or they will say the wrong thing and make a fool of themselves. These are honest concerns, but the worst that can happen in those two situations fails miserably in comparison to the worst that can happen when you don't say anything at all.

I am fully aware of the fact that men talk less than women and that it's nice to just sit in silence from time to time. But if you want to serve your friends or family or if you want to be a great husband or a great dad, then you need to speak truth to (and over) the people you care the most about. Godly, biblical, timely truth will bring life to your friends and family in a way that nothing else can, and it will help them avoid making huge mistakes or missing out on huge opportunities. So...

- Speak the truth over the women in your life (from your mom to your sisters to that special someone) that they are fearfully and wonderfully made.
- Speak the truth over your friends that they are not alone, and that they can always count on you, as well as the Lord, to walk them through the trials and storms of this life.
- Speak the truth over the Christians in your life that they have God's Spirit in them, and thus, they have the power to do more than they could possibly ask or imagine.
- Speak the truth over your own doubts, fears, insecurities, and struggles.

You will be great, and help others to become the same, when you speak truth to them.

2) Step Up To Do The Thankless Jobs

The thing about Jesus' example in John 13 is that he did

a job that no one else in the room wanted to do. It was a job anyone could have done and a job everyone knew needed to be done, yet no one did it! In that culture, feet were rather disgusting because they were covered in dirt, grime, and much, much worse (remember, power flush toilets had not been invented yet). So when people entered someone else's home, it was the servant's job to wash the feet of the guests. Clean feet helped everyone feel more comfortable. But in order for that to happen, a servant had to get his or her hands really, really dirty.

And on this particular night, the night Jesus and his disciples gathered together for what would be their last supper, no one stepped up to do it. Everyone's feet were disgusting and the basin of water was sitting over in the corner of the room the entire time. They all knew this thankless, gross, demeaning task needed to be done, but no one did it.

Except for Jesus.

The master of the universe took on the role of the servant. He grabbed the rags, got on his knees, and did the one thing that no one else wanted to do.

That's what made Jesus so great. The same will be true for us. I believe that great men are those who step up to do the work (the gross and grimy work) that others shy away from. The menial tasks, the thankless tasks, the tiring, burdening, unseen, and unappreciated tasks—those are what make you great in God's eyes. When no one else wants to step up and do it, God is so proud of that fact that you will! No, it's not glamorous. No, it's not grand. But that's where we become truly great.

I get it. It's hard to do it. You've been working or at

school all day. You're tired. It would be easier to ignore it or wait for someone else to do it. Jesus could have used all of those excuses as well. But he didn't. He manifested his greatness in the grime. I pray you will as well.

3) Strive to Move Forward And Make Progress

Great men will constantly strive to be better at any and every area in life. I'm not necessarily talking about getting better at golf, softball, or darts. I'm talking about getting better when it comes to your spiritual development and maturity. Great men will not be satisfied with mediocrity or stagnation when it comes to being like Christ. Great men will constantly want to grow in their godliness. Living in your childhood home as a young adult is one thing. But having a childish faith when you are a young adult is another.

What will make us great in God's eyes is an admission that we are currently far from it. What will make us great in God's eyes is a recognition that we need others speaking truth and wisdom (and even rebuke) into our life. What will make us great in God's eyes is a commitment to exuding more fruits of the Spirit each and every day, week, month, and year.

Greatness requires and will always include growth, your own growth as well as a commitment to helping those around you grow. Growth is difficult. It takes time and effort. It takes a humble recognition that you need it. But a desire to grow is what will make you great.

Preach It, Gaga

Lady Gaga had it right—we all live for the applause. We all want to be great. And that's because we've all been made in the image of a great God. According to that great God, the One who is the epitome of it all:

- Greatness isn't about stardom. It's about servitude.
- Greatness isn't about being manly. It's about being godly.
- Greatness isn't about being praised by others. It's about being like Jesus to others.

I pray this will be your new definition of greatness. Because when you live that way, I will be the first to stand up and give you a round of applause.

I take that back.

God will be the first to stand up. And his applause will last for all of eternity, which leads us to our seventh and final desire, legacy.

Drive This Desire Home

To really drive this desire home, try one of the following things:

Be Real

I am overly competitive. I like when others praise me. I want to win at everything. That's how this desire manifests itself in my life.

How about for you? How are you driven by a desire for greatness? In what ways (either overtly or secretively) do you want to be the best? From your sports stats, to your social media profile, to your scholastic successes, spend a few minutes diving deeper into this particular desire.

Compare and Contrast

Spend a few minutes thinking about and listing off what makes the world applaud versus what makes God applaud. Think about the last time someone praised you or congratulated you. Do you think Jesus was applauding you as well? Why or why not? Compare and contrast what makes the crowd cheer against what you think would make Christ cheer.

Shout It Out

Read the first five verses of Psalm 95 again:

> *Come, let us sing for joy to the Lord; let us shout aloud to the Rock of our salvation. Let us come before him with thanksgiving and extol him with music and song. For the Lord is the great God, the great King above all gods. In his hand are the depths of the earth, and the mountain peaks belong to him. The sea is his, for he made it, and his hands formed the dry land.* (Ps. 95:1–5)

Take a few minutes and just praise God for his greatness. I'm not talking about a weak, "Thank you God, you rock." I'm talking all-out, top-of-your-lungs, make-a-scene, exuberant praise. He is the Great King, the Greatest of All Gods. Spend a few minutes shouting out what makes God so great.

Try It

Put this book down right now and go do something you think would make Jesus stand up and say, "Whoa! That's what I'm talking about!"

Go to a hospital or a nursing home and start praying for people. Speak truth over the "mountains" that you and your friends are standing in front of, and boldly ask God to cast those mountains into the sea. Get on your hands and knees and do something only a servant or a slave would do. Do something that no one else will ever see except God himself. And do it with the same fervor and passion you would have if 100,000 people were watching. Greatness awaits, and it starts the moment we seek to please Christ and not the crowd.

---

1. C. S. Lewis, *Mere Christianity: Comprising The Case for Christianity, Christian Behaviour, and Beyond Personality*, (New York: HarperCollins, 1998), 124.

IN LOVING MEMORY OF ... YOU
LEGACY

A young business owner was experiencing tremendous success in his new startup company. He decided it was time to open a second and third location. One of his closest friends thought it would be nice to send a floral arrangement congratulating him on all of his accomplishments. When the friend arrived at the party where he had sent the flowers, he was appalled to find that his arrangement bore the inscription: "I'm so sorry. I know that things will be tough for you and never the same again."

Angry, he immediately called and complained to the florist. He argued, "That wasn't encouraging at all. In fact, it sounded insulting!" After apologizing profusely, the florist said, "But look at it this way, sire. Somewhere else a man was buried today under a wreath that said, "Yeah buddy! Go get 'em, tiger!"

Our last desire deals with life and death but more importantly, what we do in between the two. This is the desire we all have to live a meaningful life and be remembered even after our death. This is the desire we have to influence and impact others so much so that our influence continues on for years and years (if not generations and generations) to come. This is the desire we have to "Go get 'em, tiger" before, and even after, we breathe our last.

This is the desire to live and leave a legacy.

Unlike the other desires, most of us don't spend a lot of time thinking about this particular one. Unlike intimacy, love, or greatness, our desire for legacy is more often than not ignored. How many of us have spent much time (if any) the last few weeks pondering whether or not we have lived a meaningful, memorable life?

Chances are that word, let alone your actual legacy hasn't crossed your mind in a very long time, if ever. People do consider this when they are about to die. But at that point, I would argue that it is far too late. If you only reflect on the impact of your life at the end of your life, then it could be said you have wasted your life. Seriously.

Author Richard Evans said it this way: "The tragedy of life is not that it ends so soon, but that we wait so long to truly begin it."[1] Far too many people wait until the game is about to be over to really assess how they have been playing it. Far too many people wait until the time on the clock is about to run out before they start taking full advantage of the time they have left. Far too many people wait until their lives are about to come to an end before they start really thinking about how they want to be remembered after this life. But what if we are called and created to actually do the opposite?

Memorial Service

When I was in college, the book *The 7 Habits of Highly Effective People* was popular. That particular book is filled with suggestions and strategies proven to help increase your productivity and impact. I actually can't recall many of the principles (sorry, Stephen!). But the second core principle from that book has always stayed with me—begin with the end in mind.[2]

Before you begin a project or start a new venture, you need to have a clear understanding as to what the finished product or the finish line will look like. Unless you know what the target or goal is, you will never know if you actually reached it. That is not only true with home remodels or entrepreneurial endeavors. It is true for all of life. To drive this point home, the author of the book asks his readers to do something rather odd, and this is the reason I remember this particular habit.

Imagine that later today, in some church sanctuary, people will be gathering to remember your life and reflect on your death. Think back to the last memorial service you attended. But now, take yourself out of the seats in the sanctuary and put yourself in the box on the stage (I told you this was a little odd, but stay with me).

Imagine Chick-fil-a instrumental worship music playing softly in the background. Imagine the stage filled with flowers or pictures or keepsakes. And imagine your body in the coffin or your ashes in the urn. Who would be in attendance (who wouldn't be) at an event like this? What would be the overall emotion or spirit in the room? Would there be laughter, tears, confusion, sadness, anger, or joy? What would people be saying or talking about? What memories would people be sharing of you? What about your character, accomplishments, or commitments would they be commenting on?

Although uncomfortable and a little strange, thinking about your death can radically change your life. If you want people to speak well of you later, if you want people to be touched and changed by your devotion to your family, contagious joy, or your heroic acts of faith, then you have to start working towards those things right now. You have to keep those things at the forefront of your mind each and every day and not just hope they will magically be true when you get to your last day.

I find it so interesting that Jesus was constantly thinking about, referring to, and talking about his death. I imagine that at times he sounded like a real downer at the dinner table: "This is great guys, but I am going to die."

Really Jesus? Nothing changes the mood or ends a conversation quite like a statement about death or dying. But I wonder if Jesus wasn't on to something. By keeping his death at the forefront of his mind, he was able to maximize and make the most of every single day (and moment and conversation) he had up until that point. He knew his time was short. He knew life wouldn't always be the same. He knew things were going to come to an end.

And I think the same needs to be said of us. If you allow the weeks, months, and years to come and go without any thought of what you are doing and why, without any intentionality or purpose, or without any clear idea as to what the ultimate goal is, then at the end of your life you will only be remembered by a handful if people for a handful of years. At best, that's it.

Let's do another little activity that I think proves my point.

- Tell me a thing or two about your parents
- Tell me a thing or two about your grandparents
- Tell me a thing or two about your great grandparents

If you are anything like me, the parents and grandparents stuff was relatively easy to come up with. But the great grandparents stuff? Outside what I learned from that DNA test I filled out a few years ago, I don't know anything about them.

In just three or four generations, people are completely forgotten, even by their own family. That is a pretty sad and sobering thought. Because our lives typically revolve around things that quickly fade away, things that are "here today and gone tomorrow," the same will be true about our impact, influence, and legacy. Unless we are very intentional about changing that.

Let me try to say it another way. If I'm not deliberate and intentional, my future headstone will be full of one or two things. The first option is that it will be full of a bunch of logos, from Apple to Amazon to my favorite app.

Because I choose to give a vast majority of my time, attention, and resources to those things, that's what is going to define my legacy. Can you imagine, though? Walking through a cemetery and seeing a headstone that looked more like a marketing ad than a memorial? Here lies

Thomas. He sure loved his stuff. He sure loved his shows. He sure loved his shoes. Nike. Netflix. North Face.

The new RIP.

Or, instead of my tombstone being full of a bunch of logos, the other most likely option is that it will be filled with a list of flowery, sweet adjectives that describe a "nice guy" or a "good Christian." Words like: happy, devoted, committed, funny (at times), blah, blah, blah, blah.

Don't you feel like a life defined by logos or a laundry list of generic adjectives just isn't enough? Doesn't your heart ache to be a part of something that really matters and that leaves a significant and lasting (and possibly an eternal) impact?

Of course, you do. That's how God created you.

Listen to the words of the founder of International House of Prayer (the man whose book I referenced at the start of this entire discussion). He writes:

> We play a small but significant role in a very large drama, in a great conflict with eternal consequences. We are not some footnote to the script. God did not create us or the world because he was bored. He is not peering down on us as if we were a collection of highly functioning gerbils in a cage. He made us to be and is looking for people who will partner with him to bring about His very Kingdom on the earth. He made us to be and is looking for people to lead the world and partner with Him to bring about redemption and restoration and reconciliation.[3]

I don't know about you, but that makes my heart come alive. I am drawn to and fascinated by the idea that I have been created and called by Christ to lead the nations, to usher in the kingdom, and to help bring heaven to earth. I was made to partner with God to redeem, restore, and reconcile all things. Those are the titles I want on my headstone. Those are things I want to give my life to. Those are things I want to be remembered for in death. And that's true for all of us. God created each and every one of us to live a meaningful life and to leave and lasting legacy. God created us to live a life that cannot be summed up by a bunch of logos or some laundry list of generic words.

Recalculating

Think back to the last time your GPS app or maps program lost its way/connection/bearings (which always seems to happen at the most inopportune time, right?). As it is trying to figure out where in the world you are, it says something like "recalculating." In other words, things aren't right, everybody knows it, and a massive readjustment needs to be made so you don't end up totally lost. A lot of us need to do some serious recalculating when it comes to our lives and our legacies. If we continue on the path that we are on, at best our great grandkids will know our names. At worst, no one will remember us at all.

But God didn't create you for nothingness. God didn't create you to be easily forgotten. God didn't create you to be cast off or discarded. And your heart desperately desires for that to be true.

Look at what Daniel writes in chapter 12 of the book that bears his name:

Multitudes who sleep in the dust of the earth will awake: some to everlasting life, others to shame and everlasting contempt. Those who are wise will shine like the brightness of the heavens, and those who lead many to righteousness, like the stars for ever and ever. (Dan. 12:2–3 NIV)

For ever and ever. Let that sink in. You were created to live a life that is not easily forgotten, one that will be remembered forever and ever! Tell me that doesn't excite you? Tell me that something doesn't stir something deep within you? That is the life, and thus the legacy, that God created you to have!

"Well Done"

The question for us is: "How?" How do we live and leave a legacy like that? How do you go from logos to eternal lights? How do you live right now so that even after we are gone, somehow we are still a blessing to others?

As it pertains to our legacy, a great place to start is Luke 19. Luke writes:

While they were listening to this, he went on to tell them a parable, because he was near Jerusalem and the people thought that the kingdom of God was going to appear at once. He said: "A man of noble birth went to a distant country to have himself appointed king and then to return. So he called ten of his servants and gave them ten minas. 'Put this money to work,' he said, 'until I come back.' "But his subjects hated him and sent a delegation after him to say, 'We don't want this man to be our king.' "He was made king, however, and returned home. Then he sent for the servants to whom he had given the money, in order to find out what they had gained with it. "The first one came and said, 'Sir, your mina has earned ten more.' "'Well done, my good servant!' his master replied. 'Because you have been trustworthy in a very small matter, take charge of ten cities.' "The second came and said, 'Sir, your mina has earned five more.' "His master answered, 'You take charge of five cities.' "Then another servant came and said, 'Sir, here is your mina; I have kept it laid away in a piece of cloth. I was afraid of you, because you are a hard man. You take out what you did not put in and reap what you did not sow.' "His master replied, 'I will judge you by your own words, you wicked servant! You knew, did you, that I am a hard man, taking out what I did not put in, and reaping what I did not sow? Why then didn't you put my money on deposit, so that when I came back, I could have collected it with interest?' "Then he said to those standing by, 'Take his mina away from him and give it to the one who has ten minas.' "'Sir,' they said, 'he already has ten!' "He replied, 'I tell you that to everyone who has, more will be given, but as for the one who has nothing, even what they have will be taken away." (Luke 19:11–26, NIV)

The wording in this story is crucial.

The master praised the servants by saying, "Well done." They were not praised because they were well-read, well-traveled, well-dressed, well-respected, or well-versed. The master did not say to the others in the story, "Well said" or "Well put."

The servants were praised because of what they did. Well DONE! They were praised because they put into practice the things that the master preached! Their legacy and what they were honored for was based on the risks they took and the things they tried.

This is incredibly important for us to hear today because a lot of Christians are good at talking about biblical truth, gathering in homes to pray about biblical truth, or even in coming together in huge sanctuaries to sing about or listen to sermons on biblical truth. But we aren't very good at actually living out biblical truth. Although I think the Father wants us to talk about and sing about and pray about his Word, I know for a fact that, like Jesus, he wants us to "incarnate" his word and make it known and visible to the world. He wants our belief to show itself in our behaviors.

Jesus said this all the time. He very pointedly asked a group of his followers in Luke 6, *"Why do you call me master or teacher, while you refuse to actually do the things I ask you to do?"* (Luke 6:46).

It reminds me of the people who describe their favorite sports team using the word "we." As in: "We look really good this year. We are getting better every week. We came so close last year. This is the year we are going all the way."

We? We!

How many laps have you run with the team? How many two-a-day practices have you been to? How much playing time do you get? Unless you put in the work, you can't call yourself part of the team. The same is true with Christianity.

"Well done," is the praise Christians must seek. But that praise is only given to those who actually do something and put in the work. Legacies are created, our lives become meaningful and significant, and we will be remembered when we decide to take biblical principles and put them into practice. When we move from hearers to doers.

Although we don't like to talk about it much at church,

the Bible makes it clear that Christians will be evaluated and then rewarded based on the things they DID in this life (See Rev. 20:12 and 2 Cor. 5:10). And that should make perfect sense to us. Think about the images used to describe a follower of Jesus. They are all action oriented: servant, warrior, lover, fighter, bride, runner, ambassador, etc. You can't just talk about, sing about, or pray about being any of these things. You have to actively seek to become them. And your success or failure in those titles is based on what you did and how well you did it.

That Was Easy

It's easy to talk about (or even debate) what heaven and hell are like and who is going to end up in each place, but it's not as easy to take that belief and let it change your behaviors. We are called to sacrifice and walk with someone who is going through hell so that they might live in light of the hope of heaven. That's what will create a legacy.

It's easy to argue over what Paul meant when he spoke about women in the church or what definition of homosexuality he had in mind when he spoke against it. But it's not as easy to start working towards abolishing the unequal treatment of women or to see, know, and befriend those who are struggling with their sexual identity. But that's what will create a legacy.

It's easy to criticize how others are trying to address problems like racism, economic disparity, or police brutality, and to complain about what others are saying or doing about the problems that are ripping apart our country. But it's not as easy to enter into those discussions, to actually enter into the struggle, and then put forth (and put into practice) some solutions of your own. But that's what will create a legacy.

It's easy to say you care about the lost, the hurting, the marginalized, or the homeless in your city. It's not as easy to actually get to know people who fall into those categories by name, and more so to go out of your way to love, serve, and help strengthen their spirits or situations. But that's what will create a legacy.

It's easy to complain about church, only talk about what "fills you up," or what type of music, preaching, or programming you prefer. It's another to go to church every week with a selfless, sacrificial heart that seeks to give instead of get, serve instead of be served, and hear the Gospel again so you can share it even more effectively the next day at work. But that's what will create a legacy.

Our legacies are connected to what we do. I didn't say our salvation, our worth, or our place in God's kingdom are connected to what we do. Those are a given and a guarantee because of grace. Our final destination is based on who we love—Jesus. But our legacies and the impact we will have in this world are all tied to our actions and behaviors and how we live in light of who we love (being like Jesus).

So, how have you lived your life up until this point? And in light of that answer, what would your legacy be at this very moment? If you died today, would you hear the words, "Well done!"?

And we all have our moments. We all have those times when we are living and loving like we know we should. Those times when we are intentionally pouring into the people around us or sacrificially giving our time and money to serve others. But are a few moments "now and then" enough? Are legacies built off or based on a few good moments? Or is a legacy built on how we spent the vast majority of our lives?

I told you before that one of my favorite movies growing up was *Remember the Titans*. It's your classic high-school-football-team-overcoming-great-odds movie. At one point when the team is playing their cross-town rival, the assistant coach for the Titans looks at his players and says, "Tonight boys—leave no doubt!"

That is exactly what the Master says to each of us. When it comes to your legacy, leave no doubt!

Throughout my career I have had the opportunity of officiating several funerals—marrying and burying is a big part of being a pastor.

But two funerals that I did one summer stick out to me because they were about as different as they could get. One was for a man who overdosed on drugs and whose life was filled with all sorts of different addictions and broken relationships. The memorial was small, short, and it was incredibly sad because the family had to stretch their thinking to find meaningful, memorable things to say about that man.

A few months before that, I did a funeral that felt more like a worship service than a memorial service. The place was packed, and people couldn't stop singing this man's praises. It was inspirational.

One service revolved around a life that was wasted, and the other revolved around a life that was well-lived, a life that was worth something and worthy to be emulated.

You were created for the latter. You were created to live a life that matters and that will be remembered. You were created to live each and every day of your life in such a way that when you come to the end of your life, others are somehow empowered in their own life.

It's one thing to be remembered as a nice guy, a good dad, or a hard worker. But you were made for more. You were made to shine like the stars forever and ever.

It doesn't have to be weird or morbid to think about (or even talk about) your death long before it ever happens. Jesus did just that, and although it freaked out his friends a bit, it seems as if it empowered him to live every day of his life so purposefully and so powerfully. By being cognizant of his death, Jesus lived in such a way that even after he breathed his last, his life (and legacy) impacted people for all of eternity. The same will be true for you and me. Let's actually live like Jesus, starting today, so that our lives will lead people closer to the Author of Life and help them experience and enjoy the hope (and promise) of life after life.

Go get 'em, tiger.

Drive This Desire Home

Do Small Things

When we think about making a huge impact for the Kingdom or leaving a significant legacy, we naturally assume we have to do something big. Typically a lasting impact is connected to starting your own non-profit or raising hundreds of thousands of dollars or having your face on the cover of a Christian magazine. But, that's not exactly how it works.

Think back to the parable in Luke. The master praises the servants by saying, *"Because you have been very trustworthy in a very small matter, take charge of ten cities"* (Luke 19:17). Being faithful in the simple things results in being given eternally significant things.

Oh, we love the loud and extravagant acts of worship, the stadiums filled with people or the ministries that reach the masses. We love seeing thousands of people "like," participate in, or give to something. Although I'm sure the Lord is very pleased with all of that, Luke makes it clear that what God truly delights in is our faithfulness in the small things and our commitment and diligence in the hidden, unseen, maybe rather thankless things. That time spent studying, that time spent with a distraught friend, that extra time on your knees in prayer, that little bit of money you gave away, those encouraging words or that decision to turn the computer off when that raunchy pop-up popped up—all of those decisions and actions matter. That's what creates a Christ-like legacy—your commitment to doing the little things day after day after day.

Some of you are wondering what difference your small acts of faith and obedience are achieving. God says they make a huge, eternal difference. Whether you realize it or not, what you are doing now in this life will transcend and carry over into the next. Everything you do, big or little, is shaping you into the type of person who is ready for and able to handle the responsibilities God has in store for you in his Kingdom.

We don't talk a lot about the fact that in the next life, God's people will rule and reign (Rev. 20). And although we don't have time to get into all of that now, it is imperative that we remember this life is but a training ground for what God has in store in the afterlife. This life is where we learn the lessons, put in the time, and mold our spirits so that we are ready for the great assignments and opportunities that are yet to come.

So continue to do the little things that God has placed in front of you. Study, work hard, be kind, give generously, make dinner, wash the dishes, listen well, take your time, stop and give thanks, etc. It's the small things that will become eternally significant things. A life committed to doing the small things well will end up leaving a lasting legacy.

Do Surprising Things

Matthew writes:

> *After Jesus and his disciples arrived in Capernaum, the collectors of the two-drachma temple tax came to Peter and asked, "Doesn't your teacher pay the temple tax?" "Yes, he does," he replied. When Peter came into the house, Jesus was the first to speak. "What do you think, Simon?" he asked. "From whom do the kings of the earth collect duty and taxes—from their own children or from others?" "From others," Peter answered. "Then the children are exempt," Jesus said to him. "But so that we may not cause offense, go to the lake and throw out your line. Take the first fish you catch; open its mouth and you will find a four-drachma coin. Take it and give it to them for my tax and yours."* (Matt. 17:24–27 NIV)

This is a weird story, and I don't really know all that's going on here, but I am intrigued by what Jesus asked Peter to do. Jesus could have just handed Peter some money and said, "Here, pay the tax with this." He could have created some money out of thin air or even pulled the old coin behind the ear trick:"Peter, wait, what's this? It's the temple tax behind your ear!"

But he didn't.

Instead Jesus asked Peter to do something surprising. It required faith and risk, and it looked rather foolish: *"Go catch a fish and pull some money out of its mouth to pay our taxes."* (Matt. 17:27). If that didn't surprise Peter, then I'm not sure what would have. And although this seems like a rather odd request at best and a total waste of time at worst, I think there is a deeper truth in the request.

Could it be that you begin to impact this world in significant ways when you begin to do that which breaks the norm, goes beyond logic, and pushes the envelope of possibility? Isn't that exactly what biblical faith should do? Think about marching around the fortified city of Jericho for seven days or getting out of the boat and walking on the water for seven seconds. Think about trusting God as you walk up the mountain to sacrifice your own son or as you stand in the flames of the furnace because of your faith. I don't know about you, but unlike the people in Scripture, I play it safe. I say I trust God and yet, I never actually do anything that requires much trust in God.

So what would it look like to go do something crazy and surprising? Something that requires God to show up? What is your fish? Where is your tax?

- Maybe it means finally confessing your sins (yes

your deepest, darkest sins) to another person of
faith.

- Maybe it looks like turning off the TV and leading
  your friends, family, or roommates in a Bible
  study.
- Maybe it means spending your vacation on the
  mission field.
- Maybe it means randomly paying for people's
  meals when you are out to eat.
- Maybe it means randomly praying for people you
  run into on the street.

I believe that one of the very best things others could
and should say about Christians is, "That was different. That was weird. Didn't think you would do that. Didn't
see that one coming." If you want to live and leave a legacy,
then you are going to have to do some things that will
surprise you and that will surprise others.

Do Spectacular Things

Although this might just be a very convenient way to wrap
up this book, I think the spectacular has everything to do
with looking to God to satisfy the deepest desires of our
hearts. You want to be remembered? You want your life to
matter? You want to live and leave a legacy? Then delight in
God above all other things and ask him to grant you and
give you the desires that burn deep within your soul.

- Believe that God is the most fascinating being
  who does the most fascinating things both in the

physical and spiritual realms. And then take him up on his invitation to be a part of those things. That is spectacular.

- Proclaim and exemplify the truth that beauty is imparted and given to us by God, and that everlasting beauty has very little to do with our physical appearance. That is truly spectacular.
- Cling to and be changed by the reality that God loves you unconditionally and uncontrollably. That is truly spectacular.
- Don't settle for cheap, fake forms of intimacy that the world pushes on you, but instead enter into God and allow him to enter into you through prayer and baptism and communion. That is spectacular.
- Give God your best and your all and not simply your leftovers. That is truly spectacular.
- Humble yourself and wash the dirty, undeserving feet of those around you. That is truly spectacular.

Someone who finds satisfaction to the core desires of their heart in/through Christ and Christ alone, is someone who will live and leave a legacy. Someone who doesn't just declare a belief in God, but who actually delights in God is someone who will live and leave a legacy. Someone who knows that God doesn't want to simply save them, but that he actually has the ability to truly and eternally satisfy them is someone who will live and leave a legacy.

Will you choose—today and every day thereafter—to seek God first, walk down the narrow road, remain committed no matter the cost, give even when it hurts, and delight in God more than anything else? Will you seek to be a person whose life shines with the light of Christ now, so that your life will shine like a star in the sky forever?

How will your story end? What will people say about your life? What will your desires drive you to do? Who will your desires drive you to become?

What you do right now—in this moment, on this day, as you put this book down—will determine all of those other things.

---

1. Richard Evans, "The Tragedy Of Life Is Not That It Ends So Soon, ..." Sermon Central, December 12, 2005. https://www.sermoncentral.com/sermon-illustrations/22949/the-tragedy-of-life-is-not-that-it-ends-so-soon-by-sermoncentral.
2. Stephen Covey, The 7 Habits of Highly Effective People, (London: Simon & Schuster, 1999).
3. Mike Bickle and Deborah Hieber, The Seven Longings of the Human Heart, (Kansas City, MO: Forerunner Books), 2006.

CONCLUSION

Like Post Malone, I'm not good at goodbyes, so let's keep this short and sweet.

Your heart burns with what seems to be insatiable desires. These are desires for things like love, intimacy, beauty, greatness, adventure, devotion, and legacy. Although these desires drive us to do a ton of things (some really good and others not so much), every single one of them is designed to drive you closer to God. The depths of your desire is matched only by the ability and willingness of our infinite God to satisfy you in those ways.

I pray something in the pages of this book awakened your heart and spirit to the reality that your desires were given to you by God. They are what it means to be made in the image of God, and they are the greatest ways you can connect to and experience God.

Go tell someone about this great God and his incredible promise to satisfy the desires of our heart. That truth forever changed my life, and I hope it will do the same for you and those you care the most about.

I'd love to connect with you, hear your story, and share more of mine at www.drivenbydesire.online

ALSO BY WHITE BLACKBIRD BOOKS

Follow whiteblackbirdbooks.pub for titles and releases.

ABOUT WHITE BLACKBIRD BOOKS

White blackbirds are extremely rare, but they are real. They are blackbirds that have turned white over the years as their feathers have come in and out over and over again. They are a redemptive picture of something you would never expect to see but that has slowly come into existence over time.

There is plenty of hurt and brokenness in the world. There is the hopelessness that comes in the midst of lost jobs, lost health, lost homes, lost marriages, lost children, lost parents, lost dreams, loss.

But there also are many white blackbirds. There are healed marriages, children who come home, friends who are reconciled. There are hurts healed, children fostered and adopted, communities restored. Some would call these events entirely natural, but really they are unexpected miracles.

The books in this series are not commentaries, nor are they meant to be the final word. Rather, they are a collage of biblical truth applied to current times and places. The authors share their poverty and trust the Lord to use their words to strengthen and encourage his people. Consider these books as entries into the discussion.

May this series help you in your quest to know Christ as he is found in the Gospel through the Scriptures. May you look for and even expect the rare white blackbirds of God's redemption through Christ in your midst. May you be thankful when you look down and see your feathers have turned. May you also rejoice when you see that others have been unexpectedly transformed by Jesus.

Made in the USA
Monee, IL
10 May 2021

67246709R00111